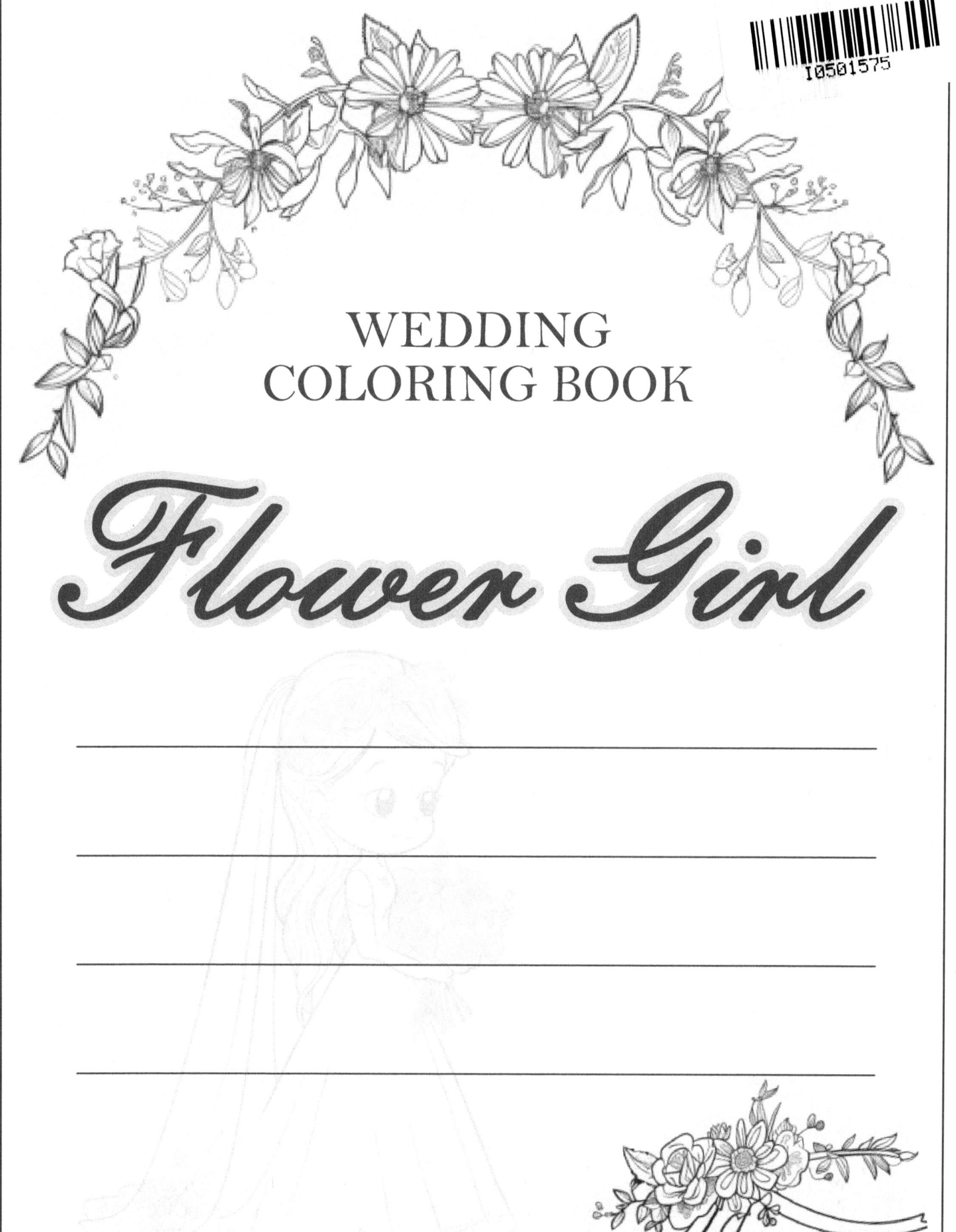

© Xaya Publishing. All rights Reserved.
No part of this publication may be reproduced, distributed or transmitted in any form or be any means,
including photocopying, recording or other electronic or mechanical method, without prior written
permission of the publisher,except in the case of brief quotation embodied in critical reviews
and certain other noncommercial uses permitted by copyright law.

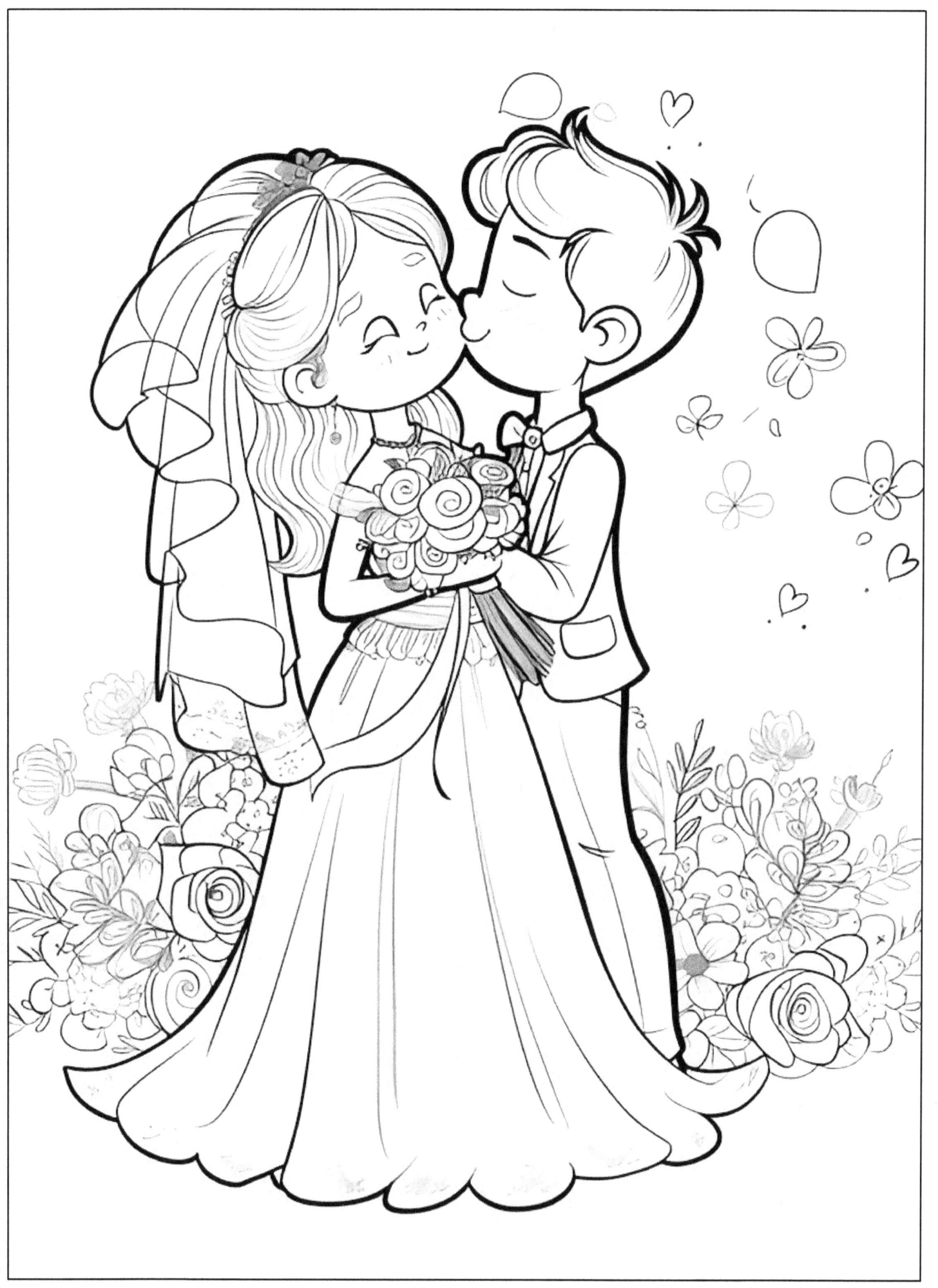

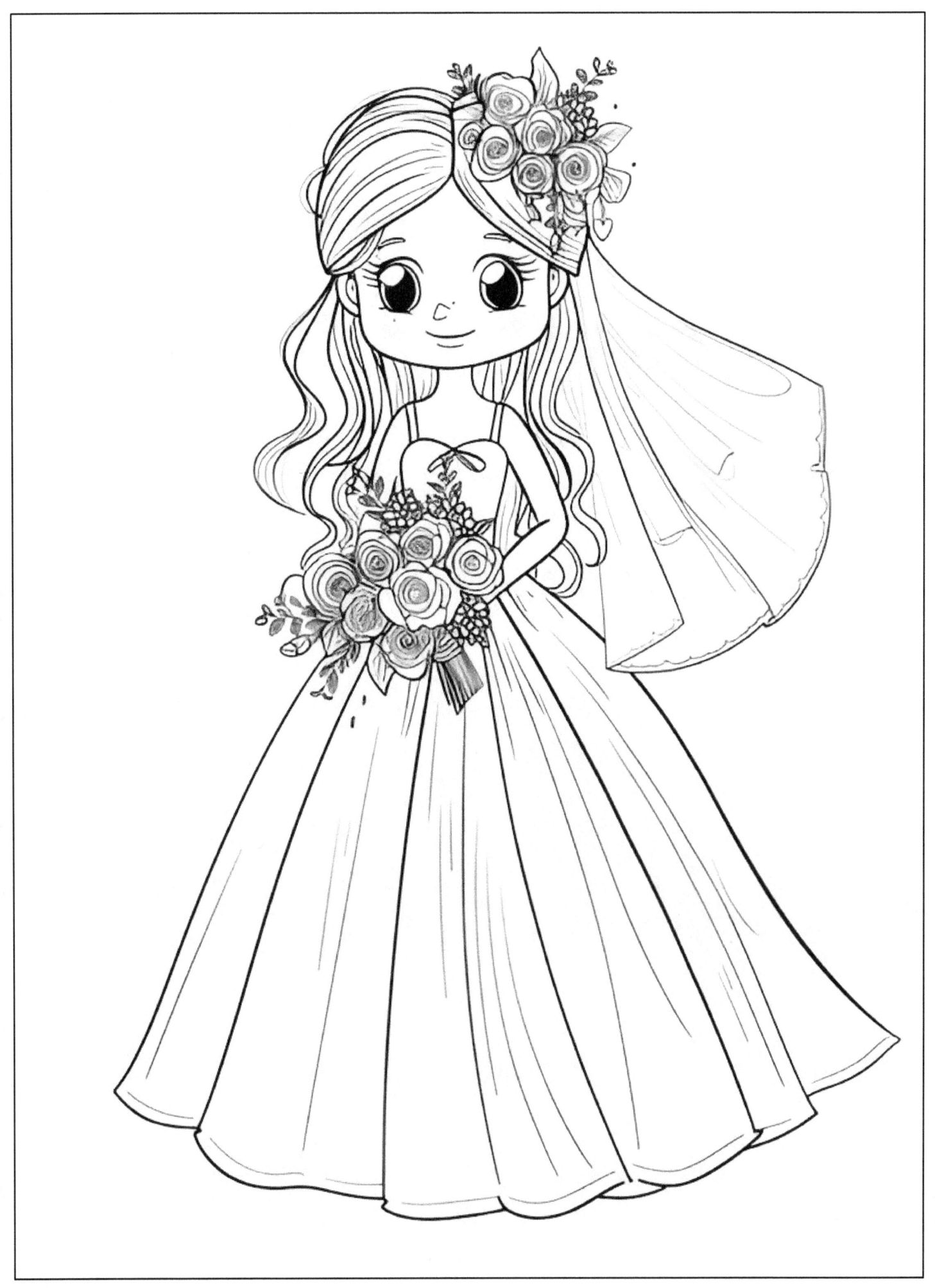

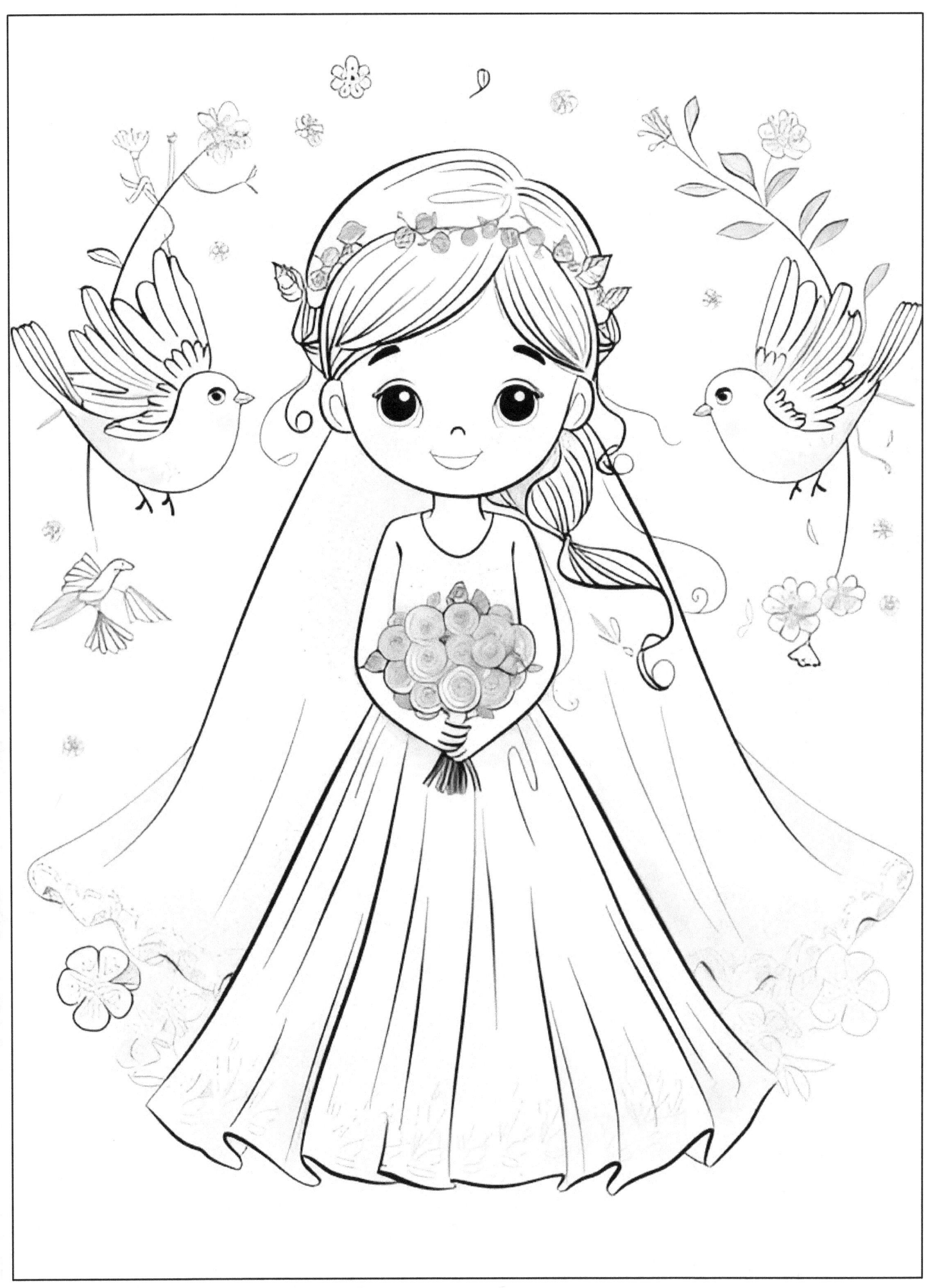

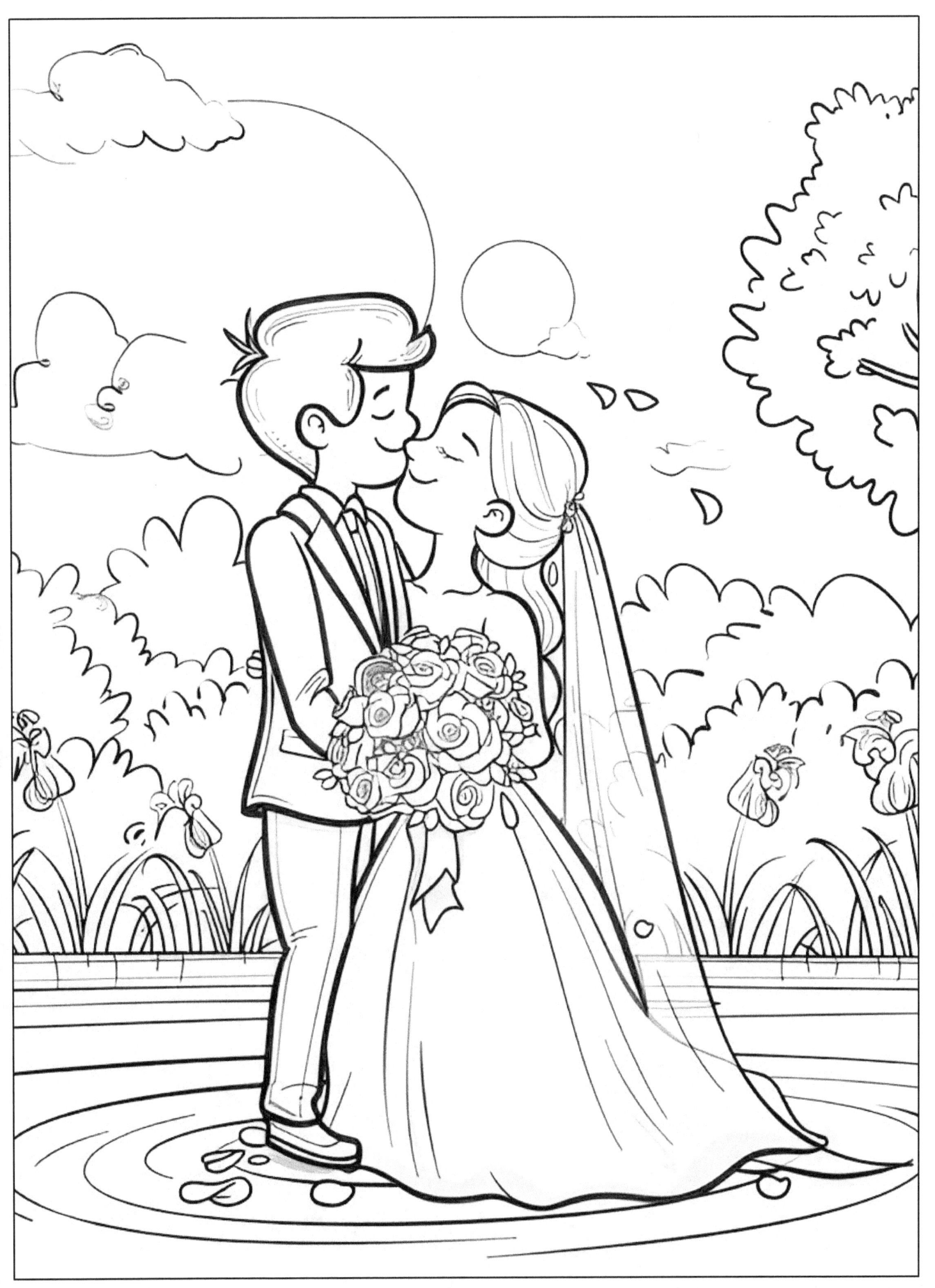

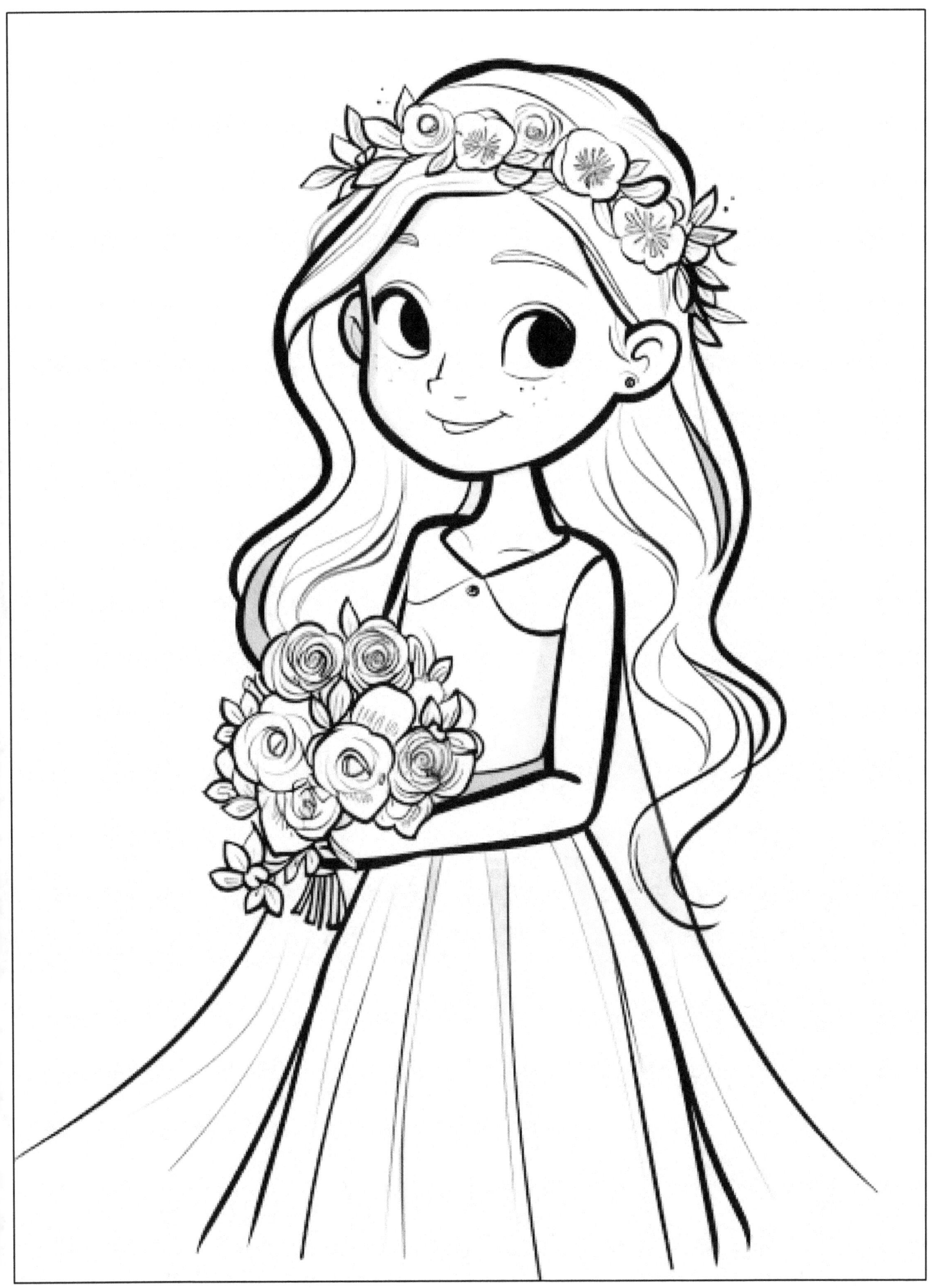

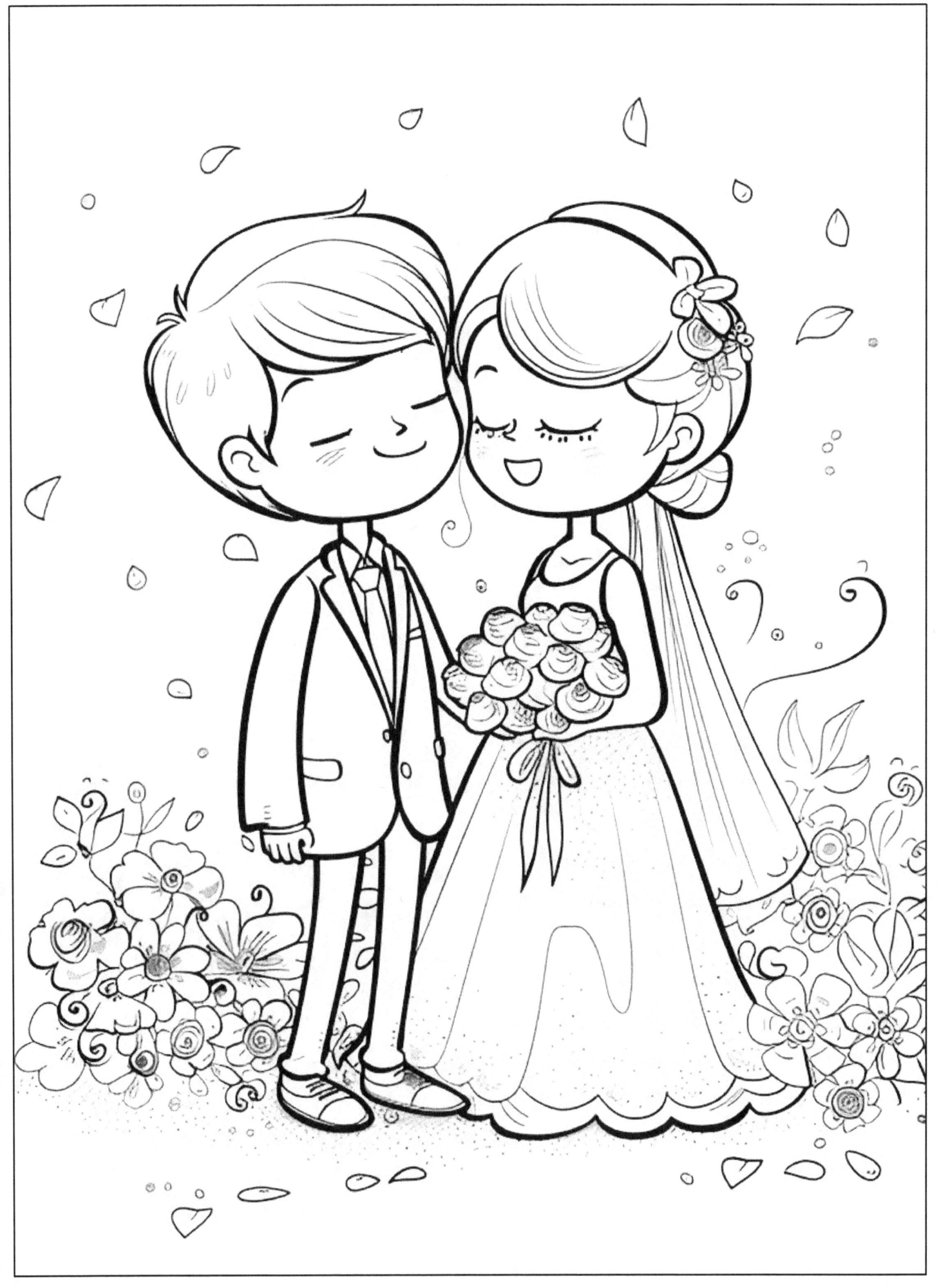

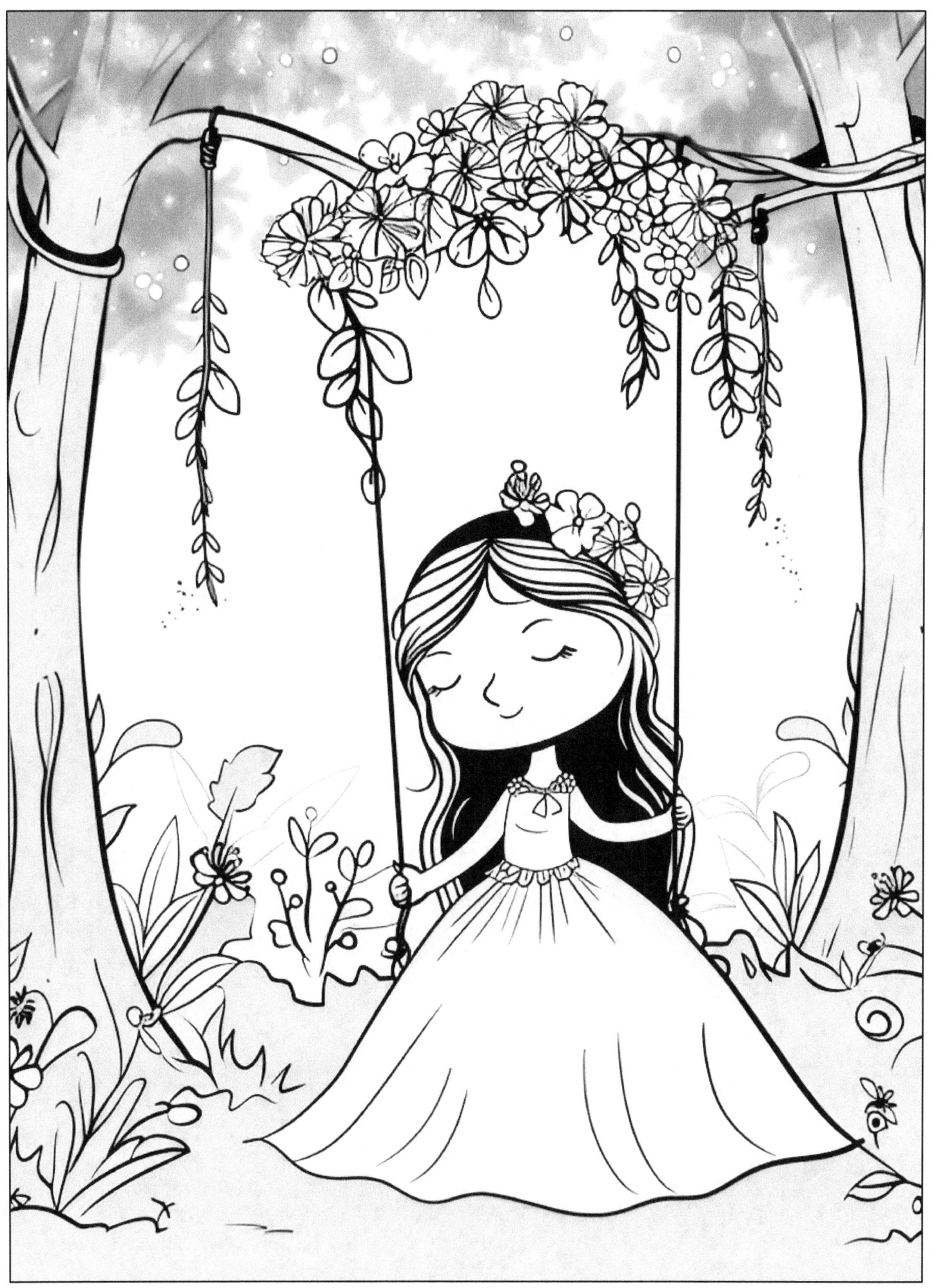

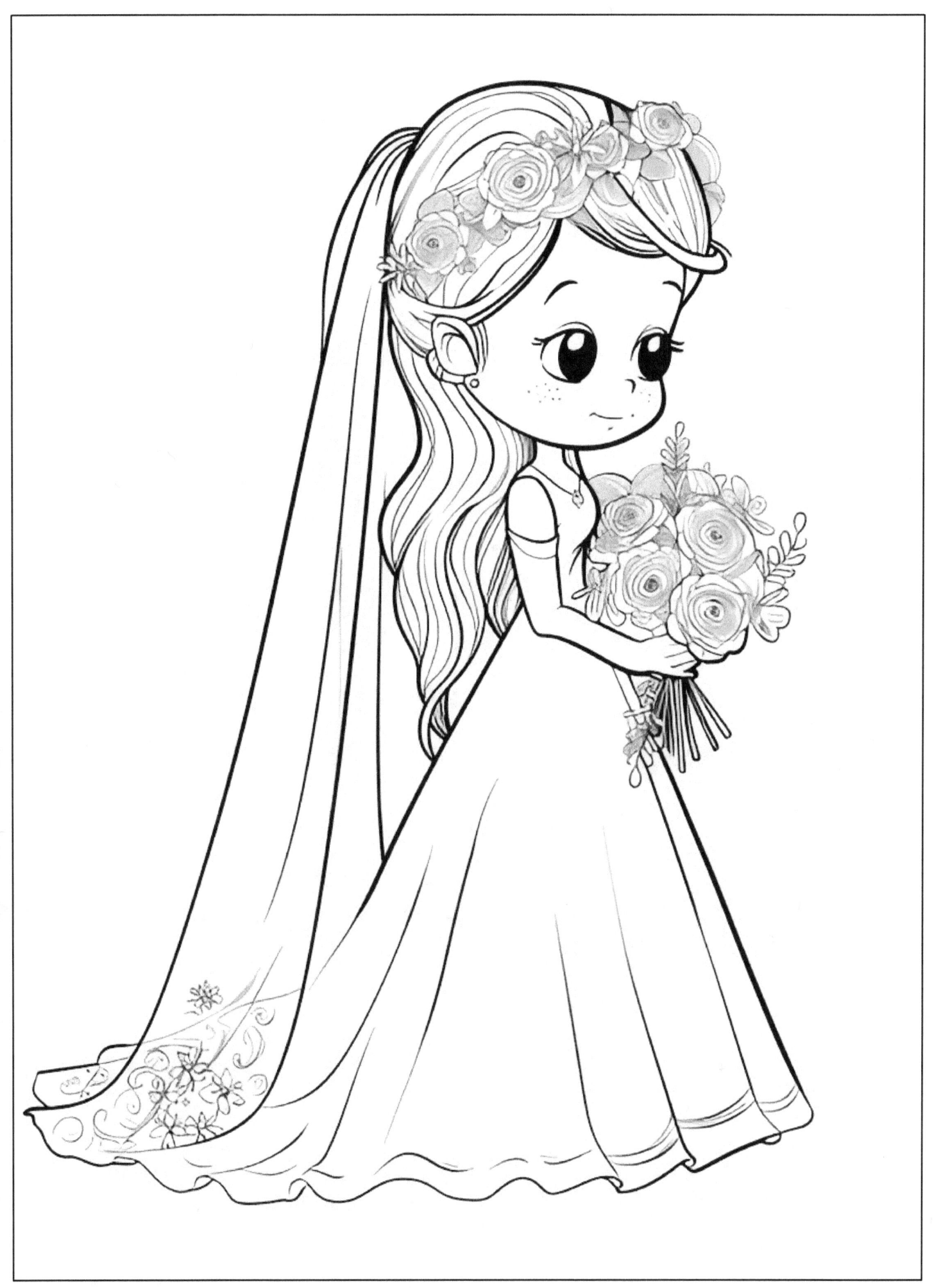

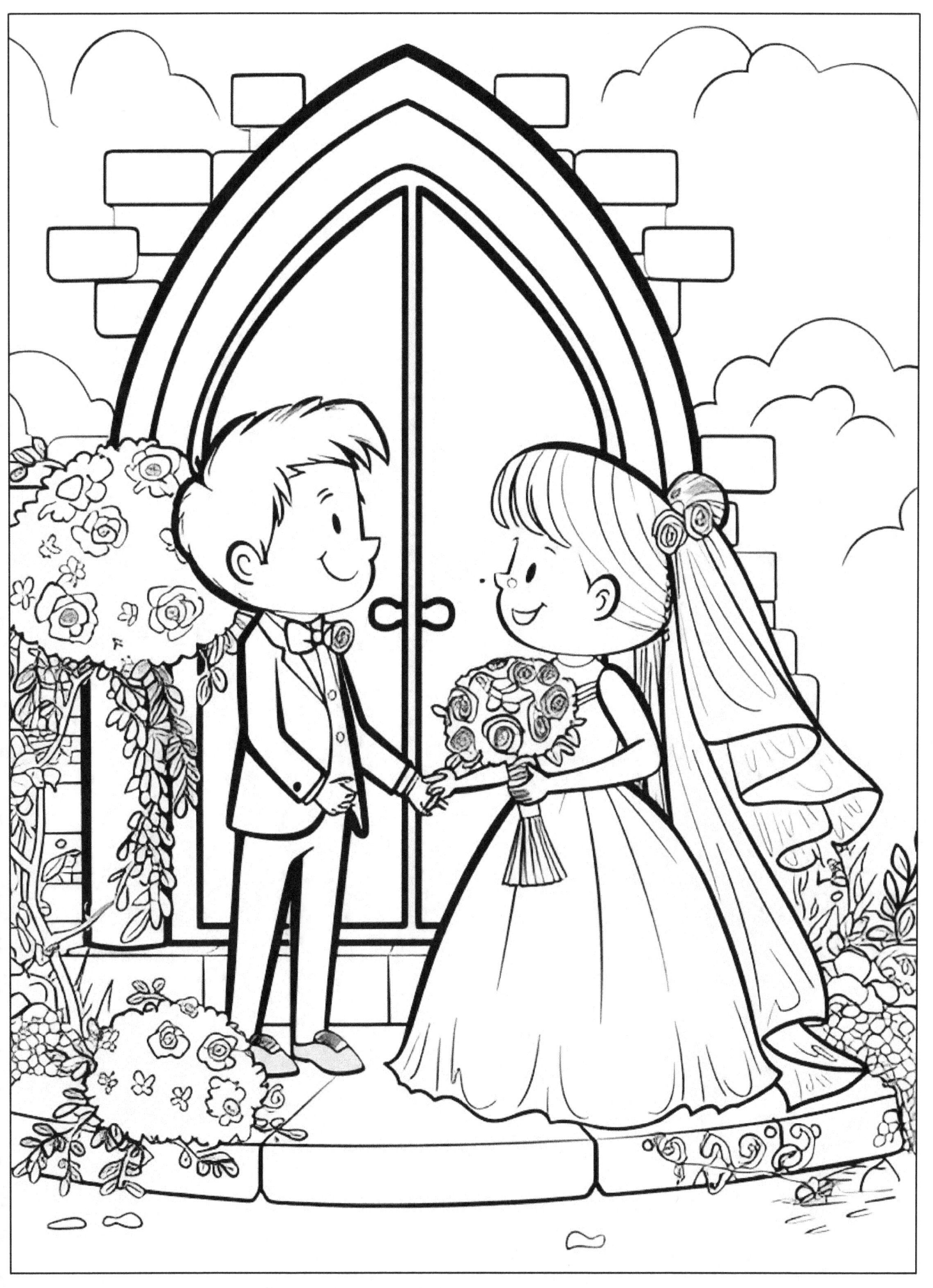

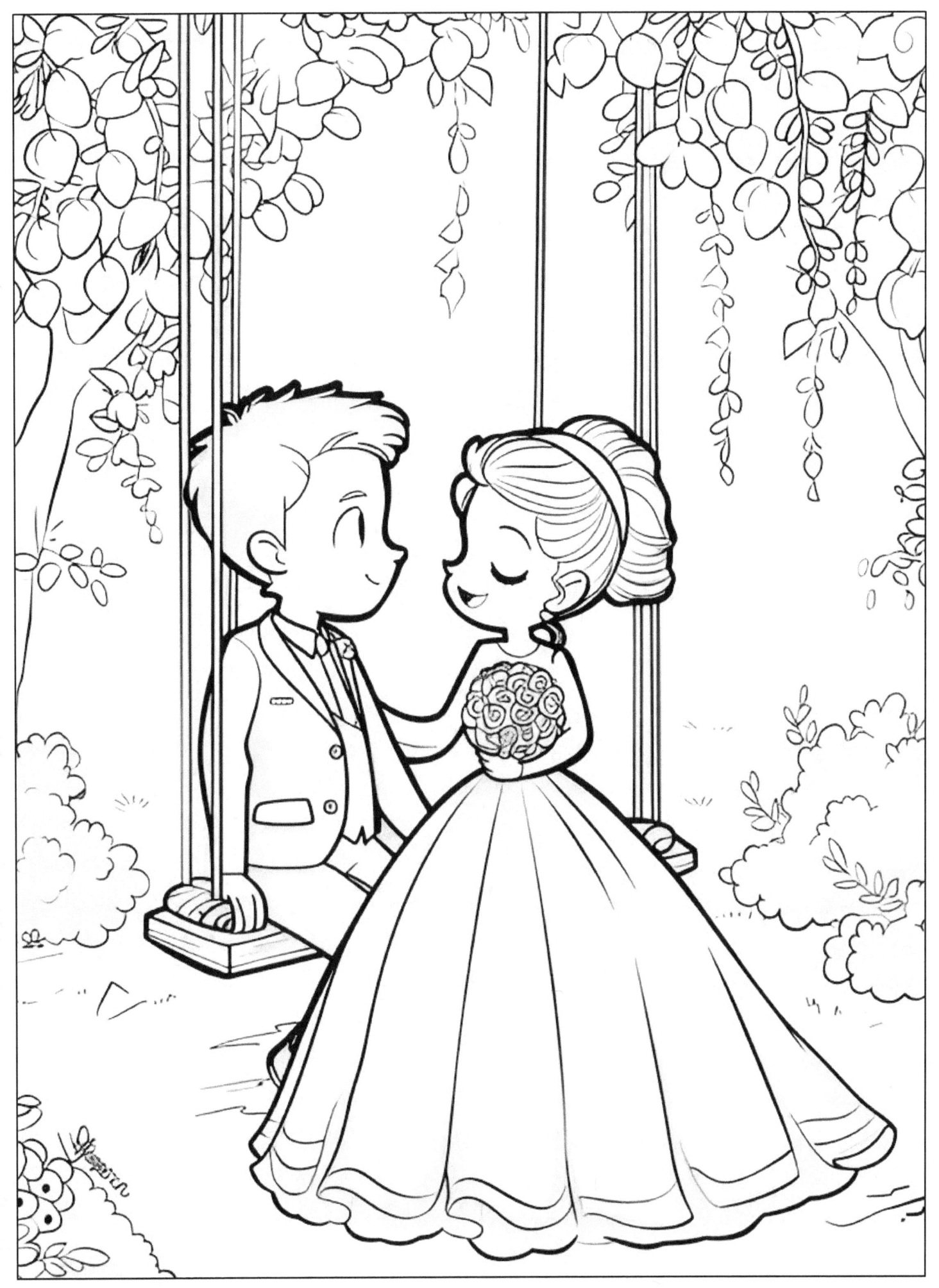

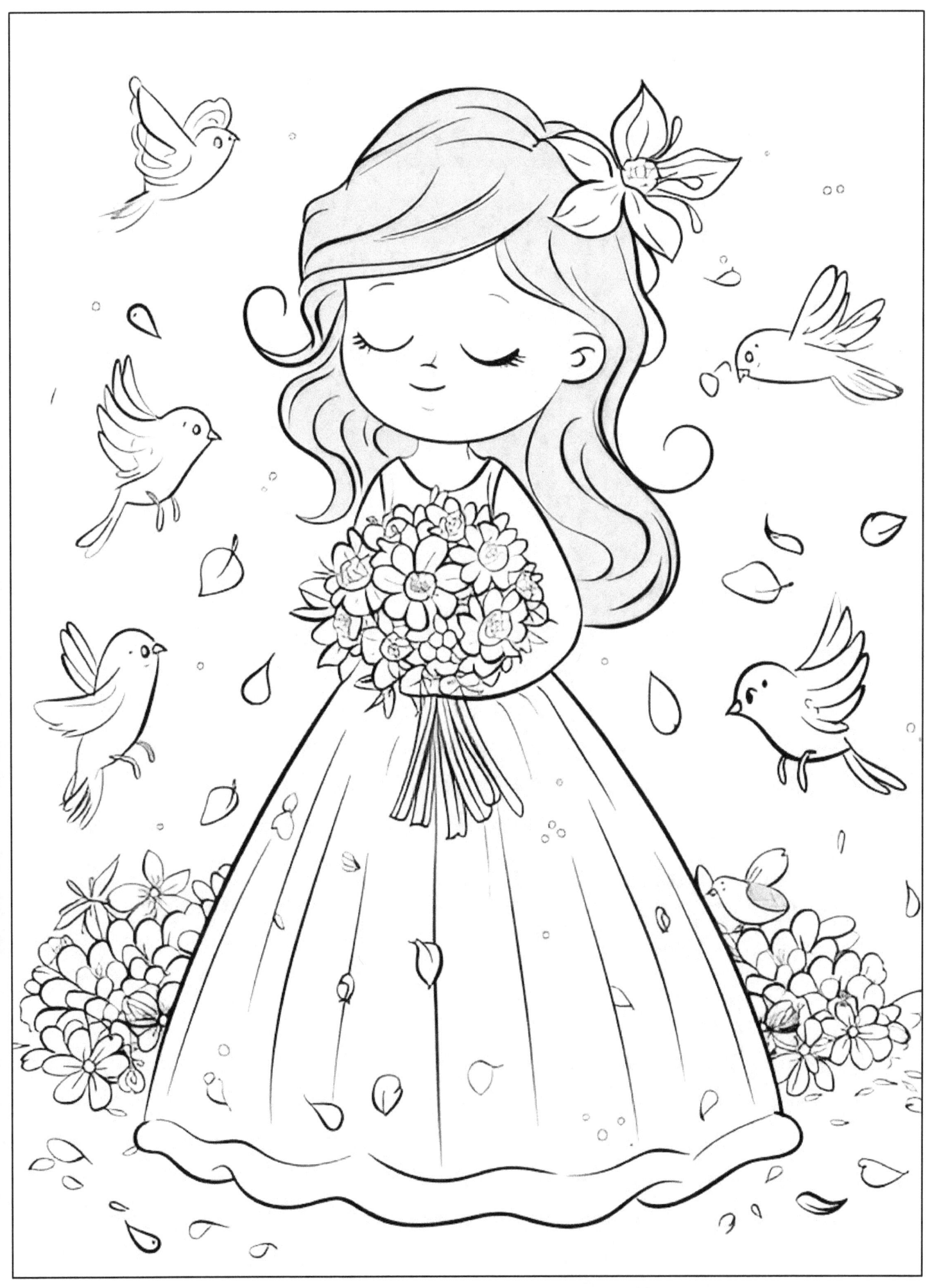

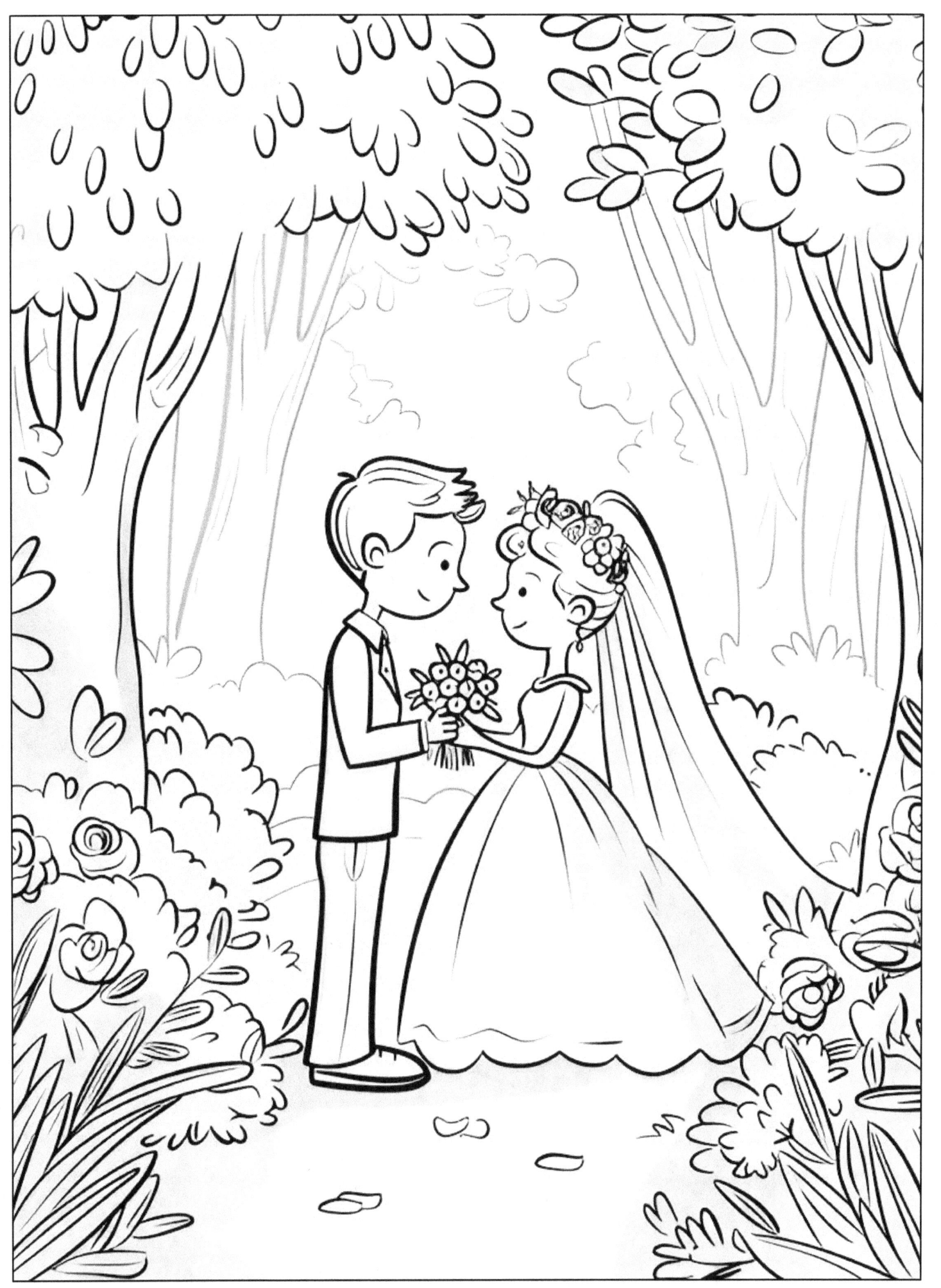

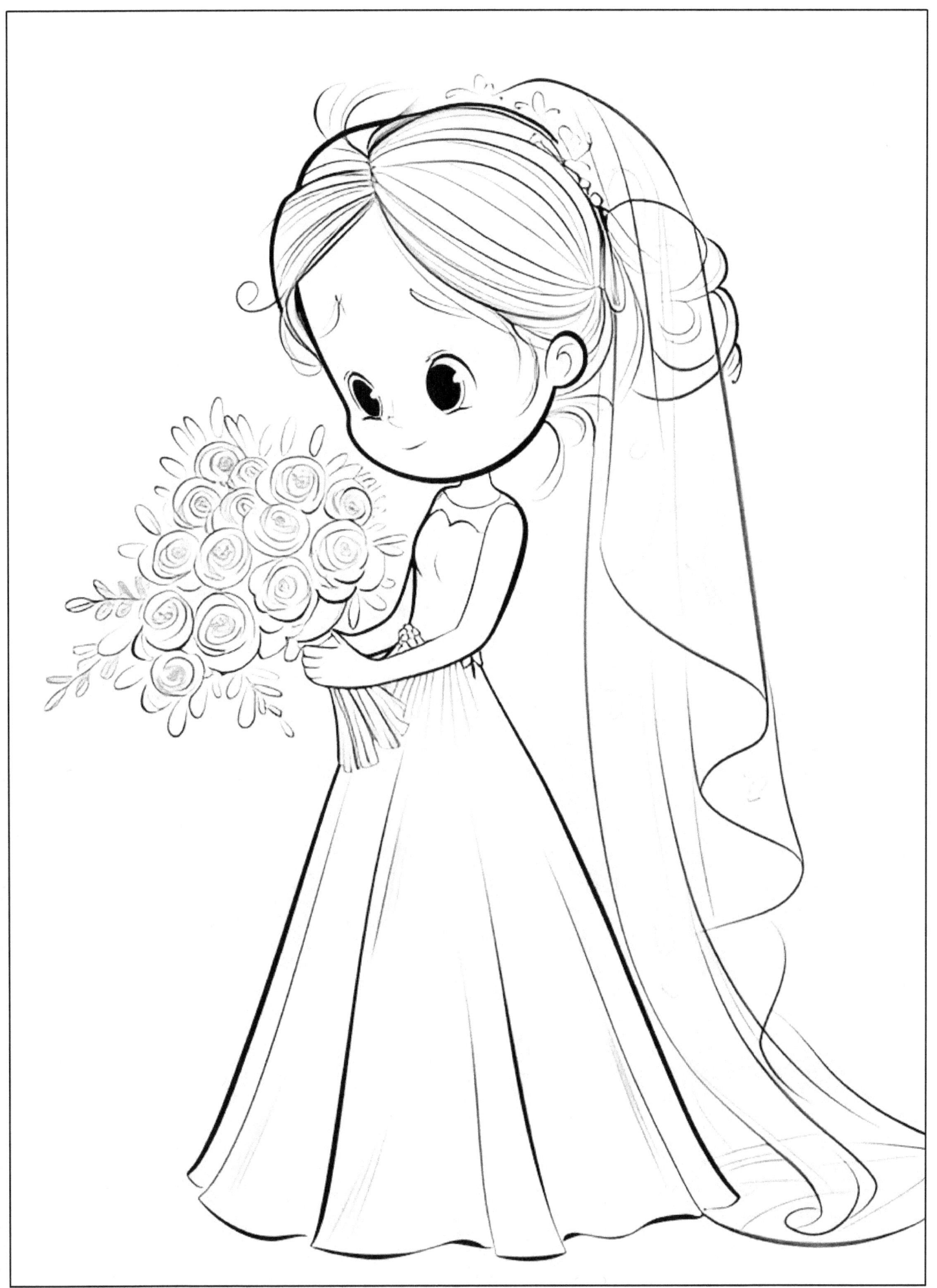

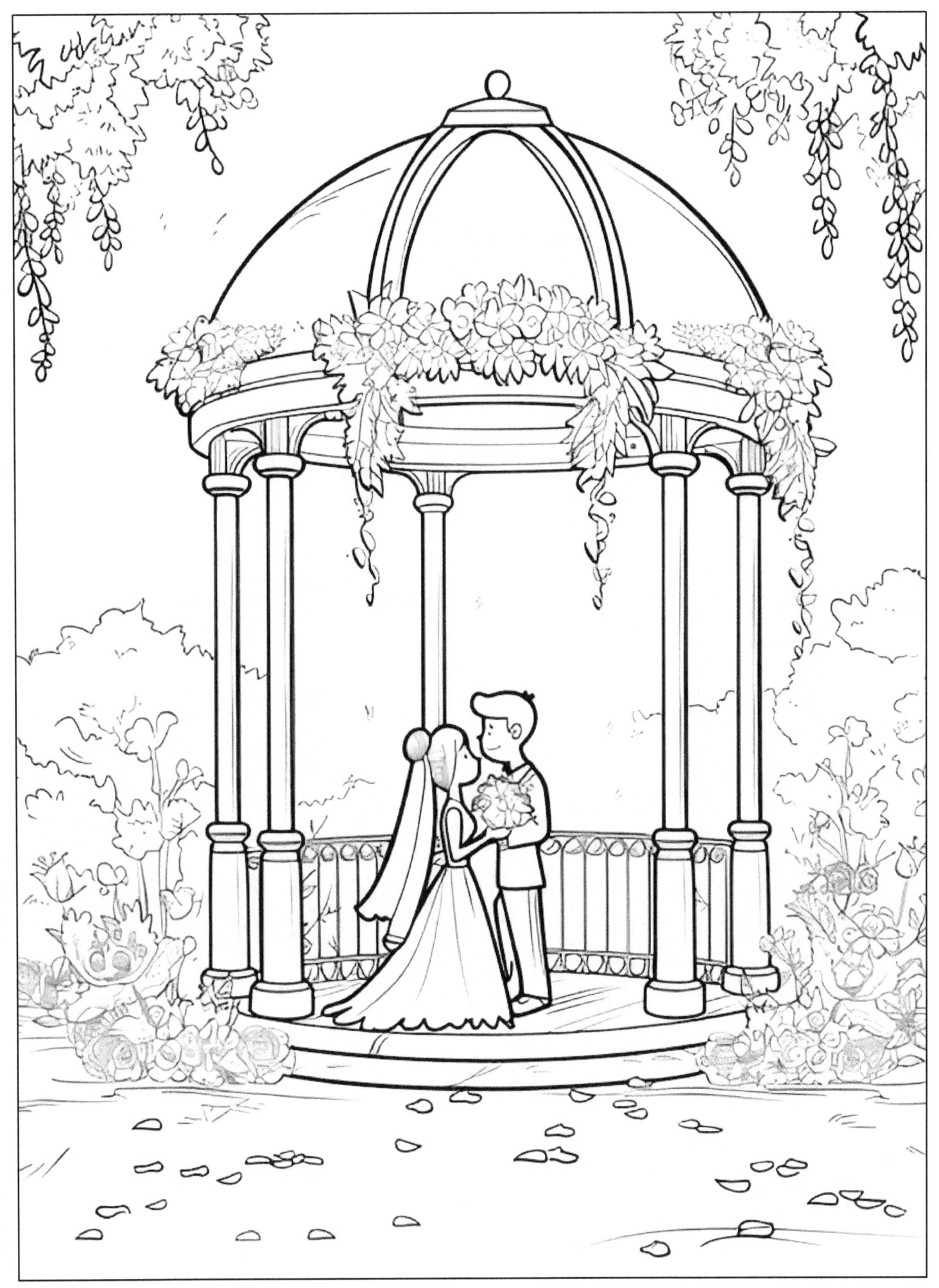

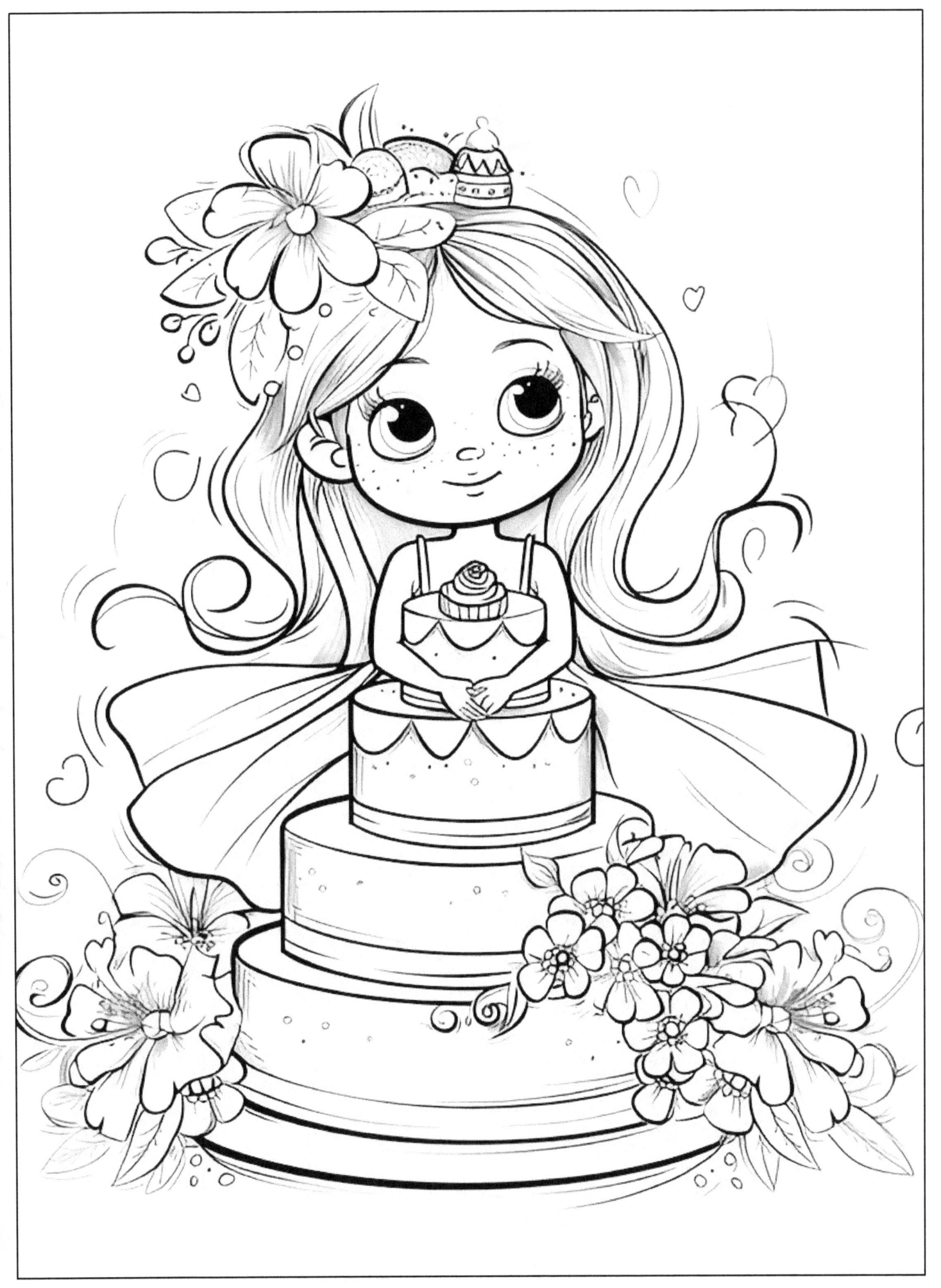

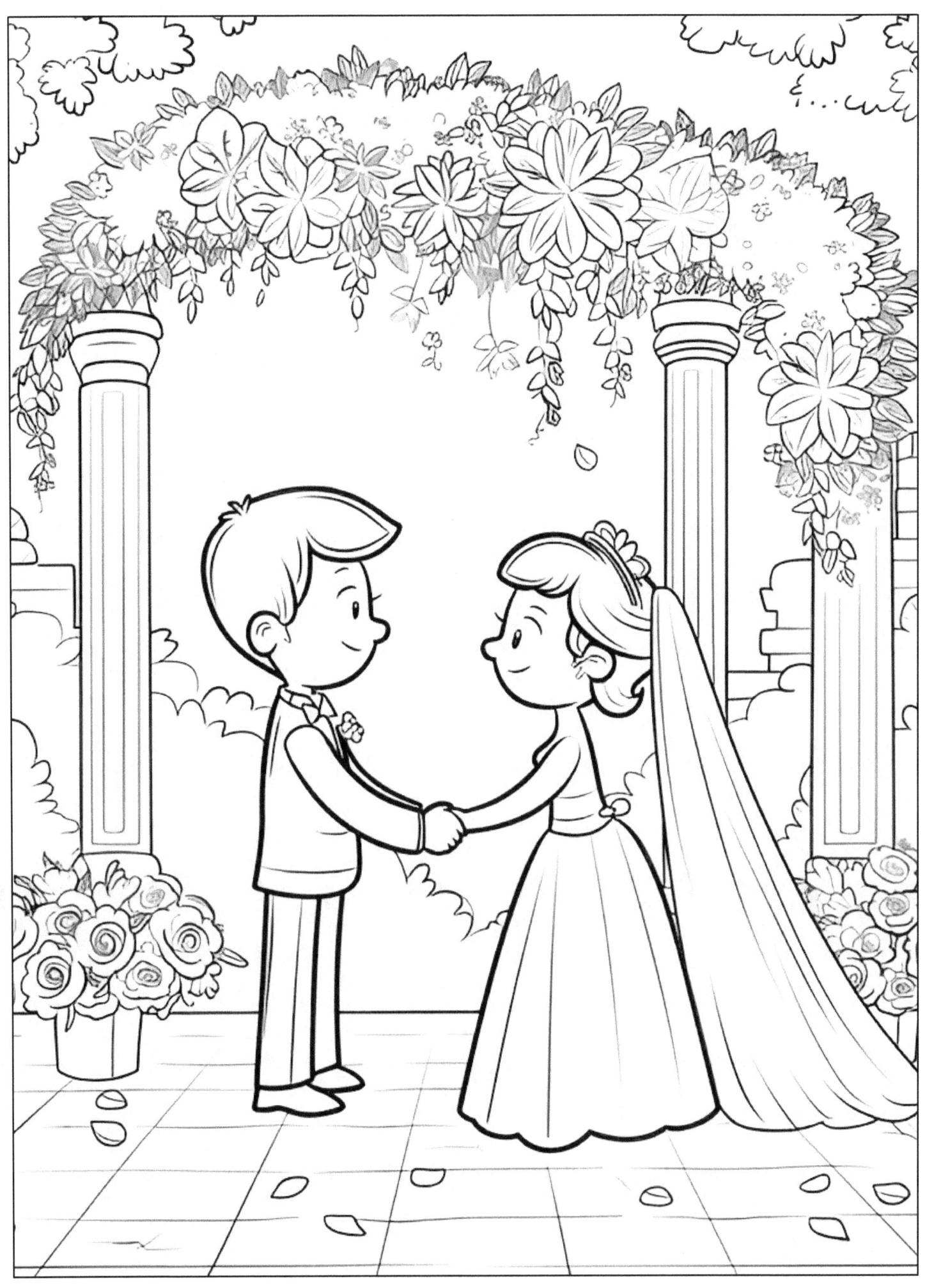

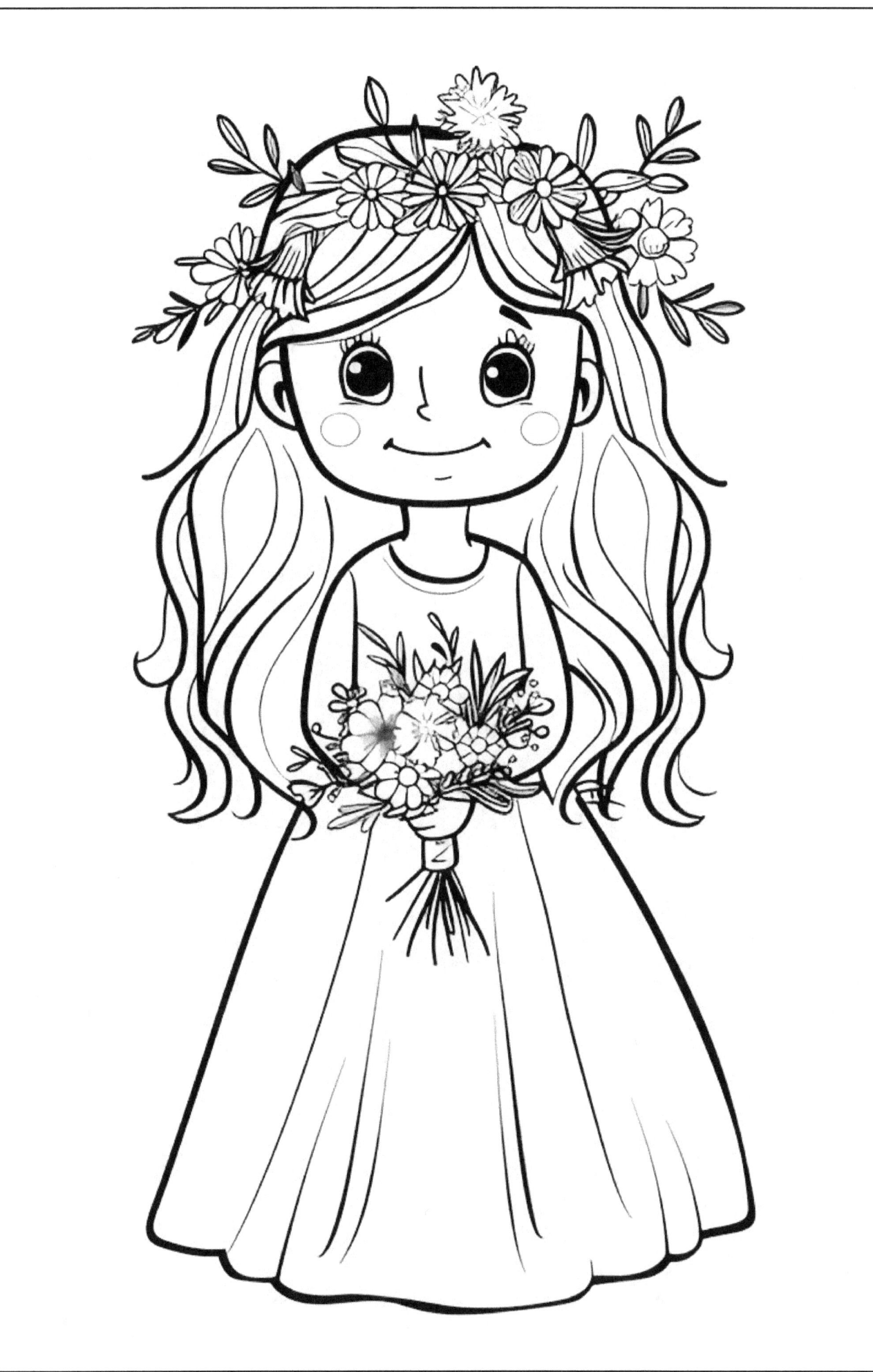

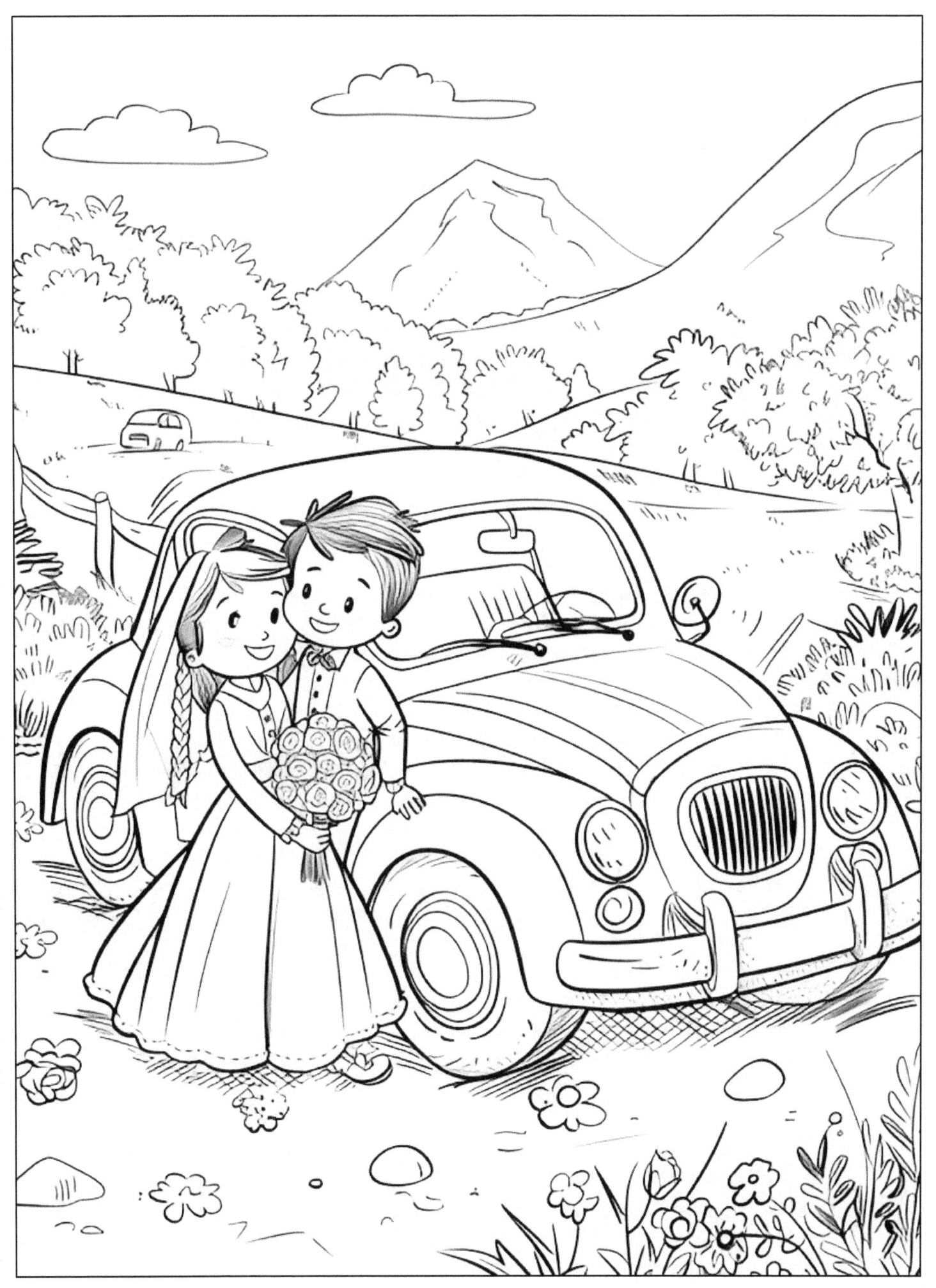

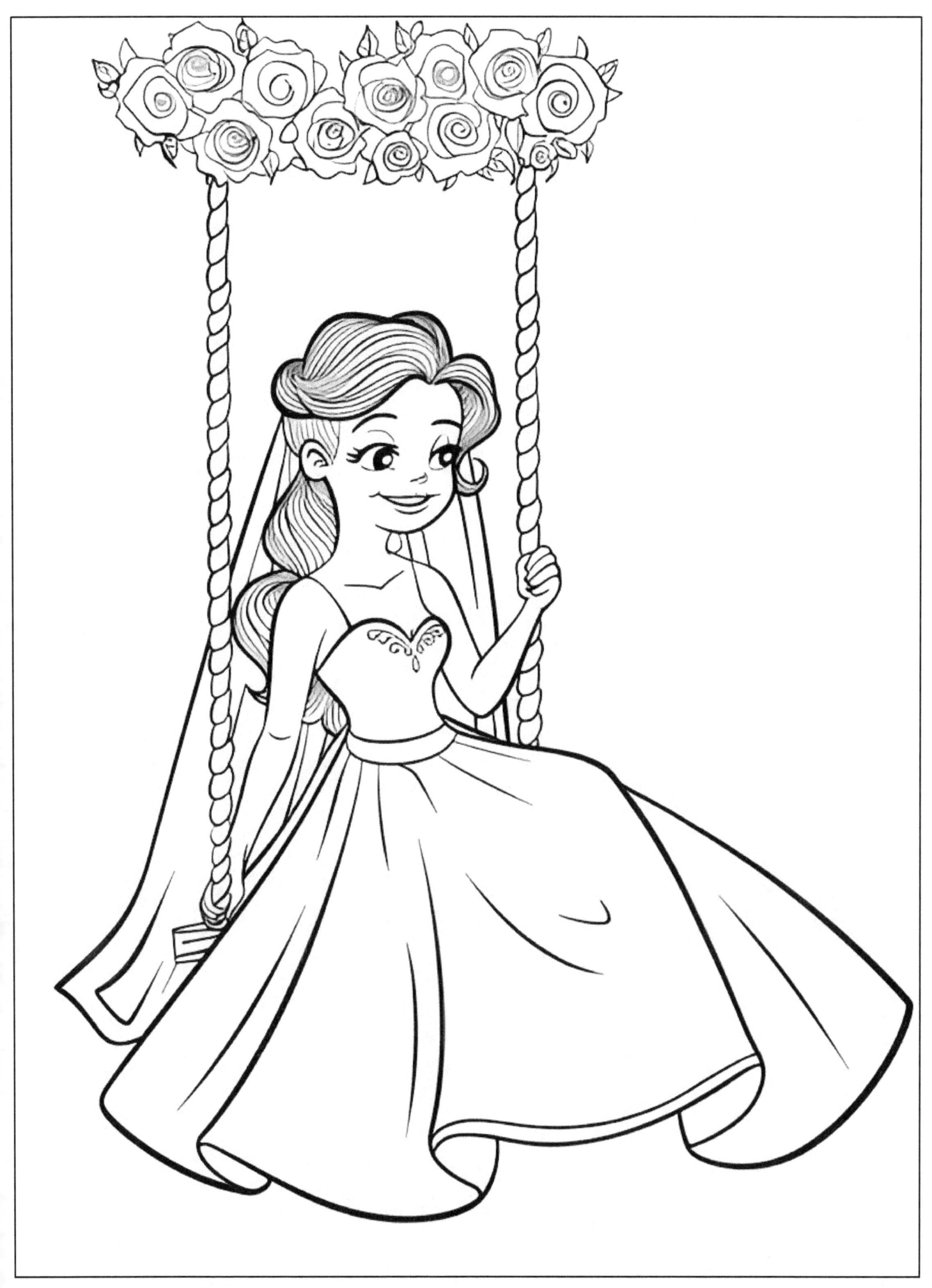

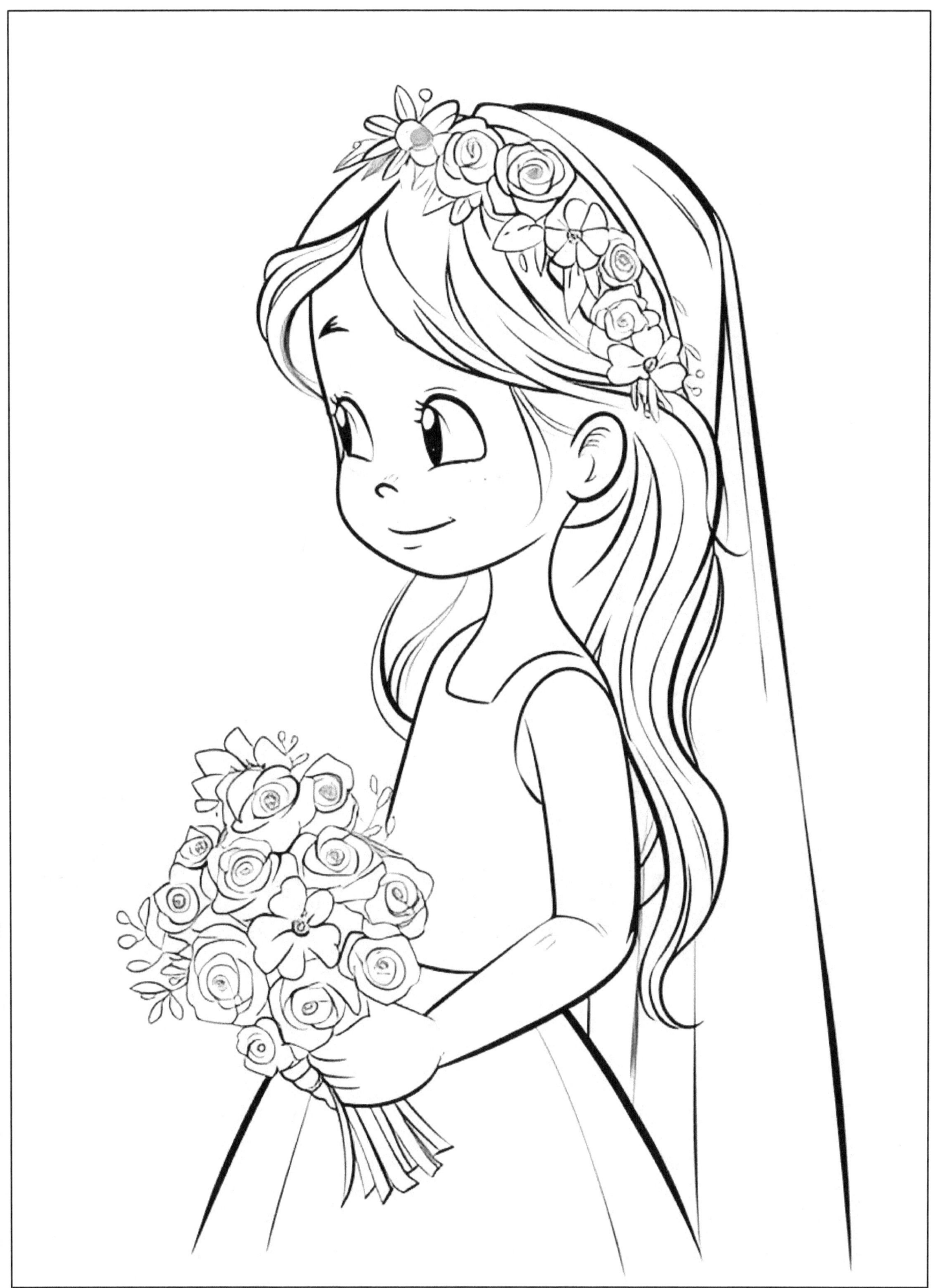

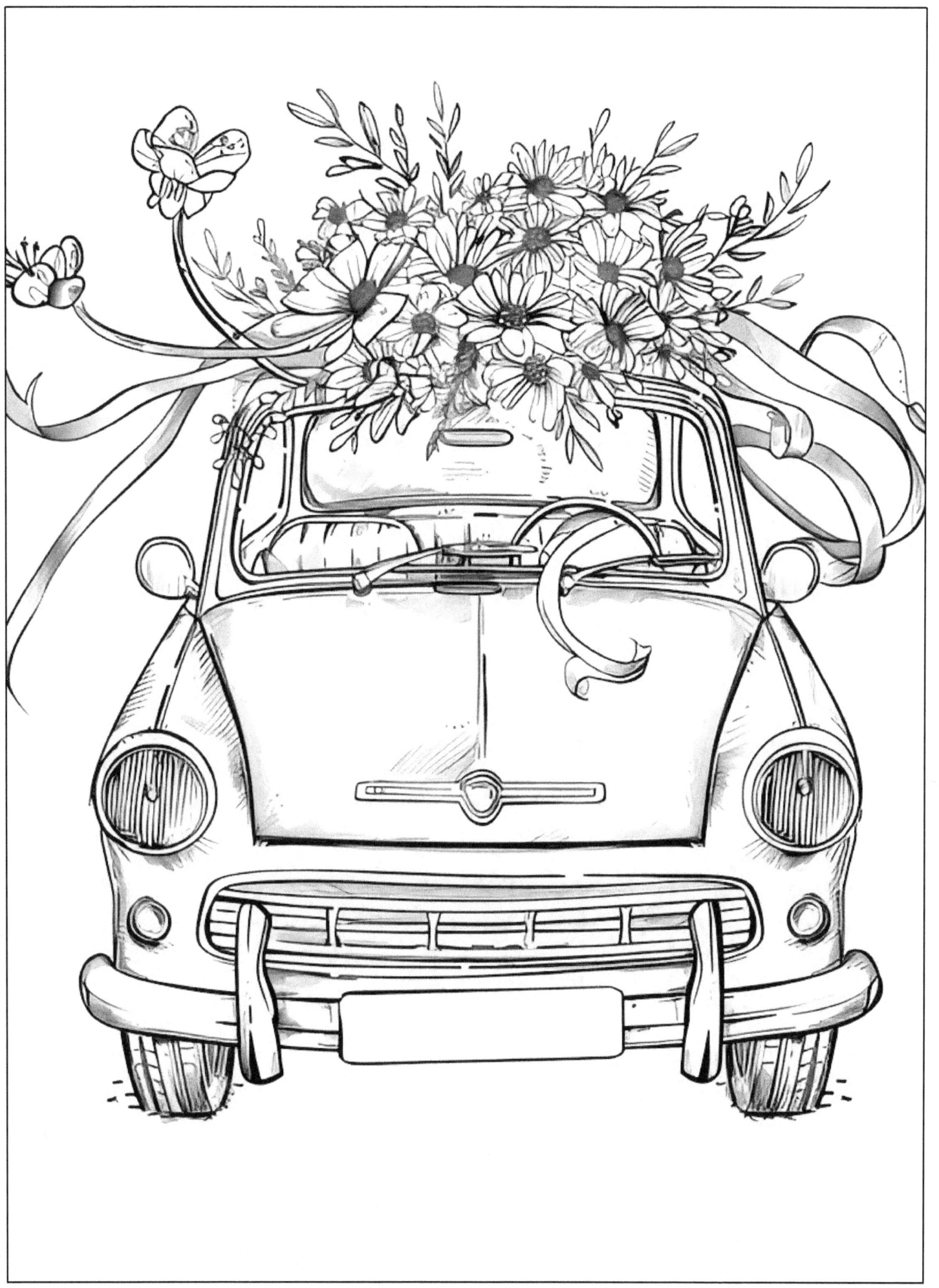

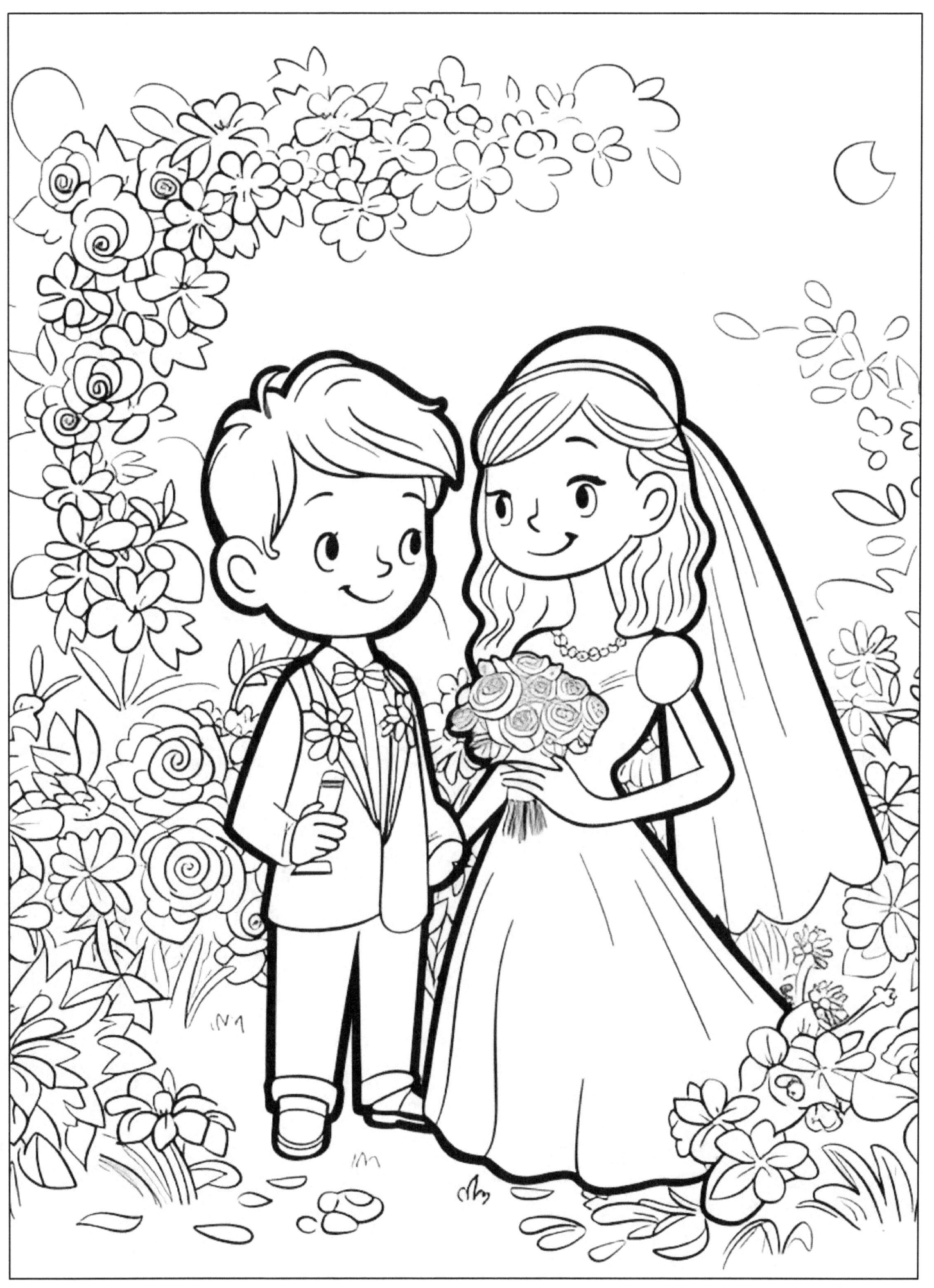

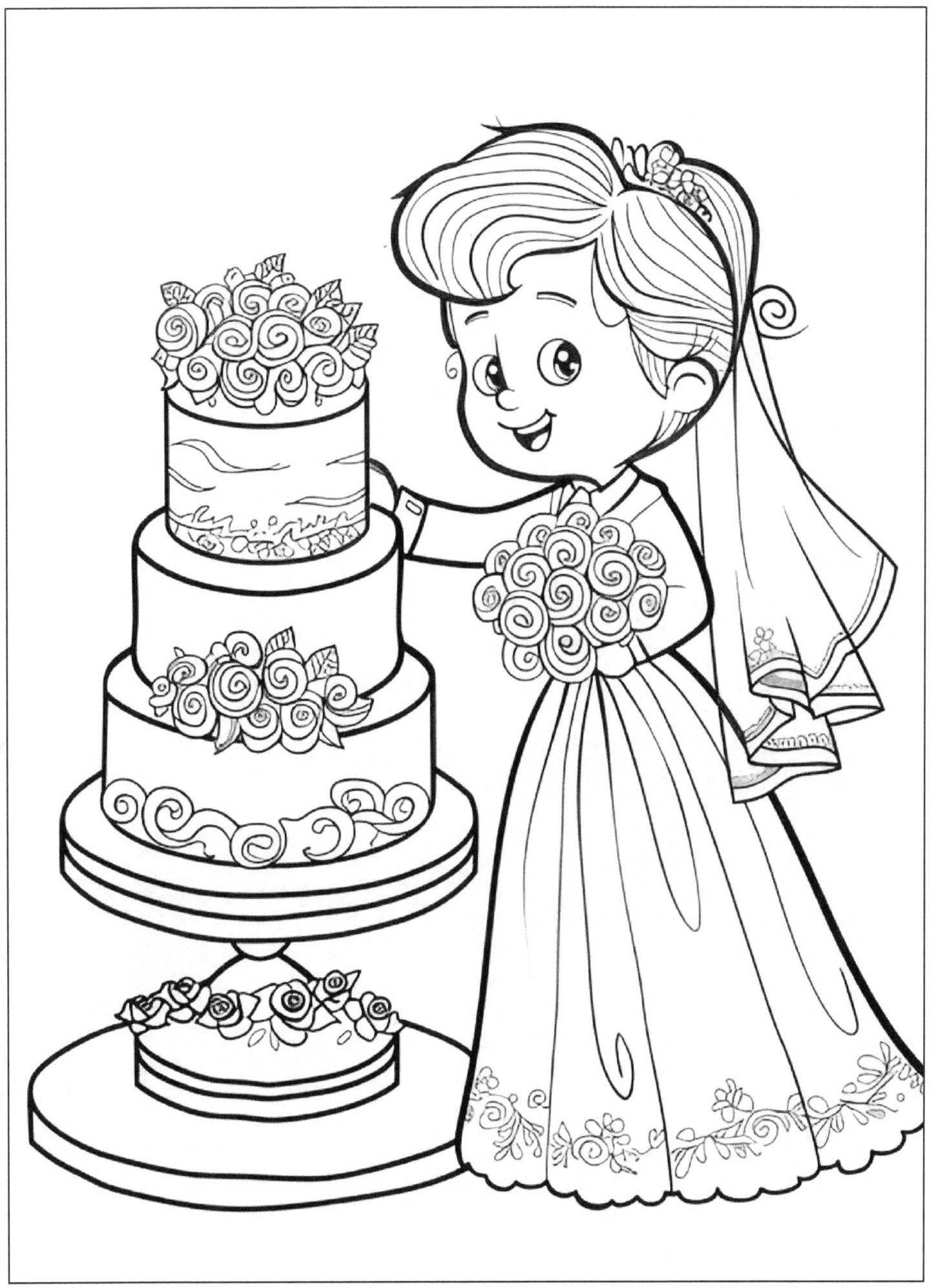

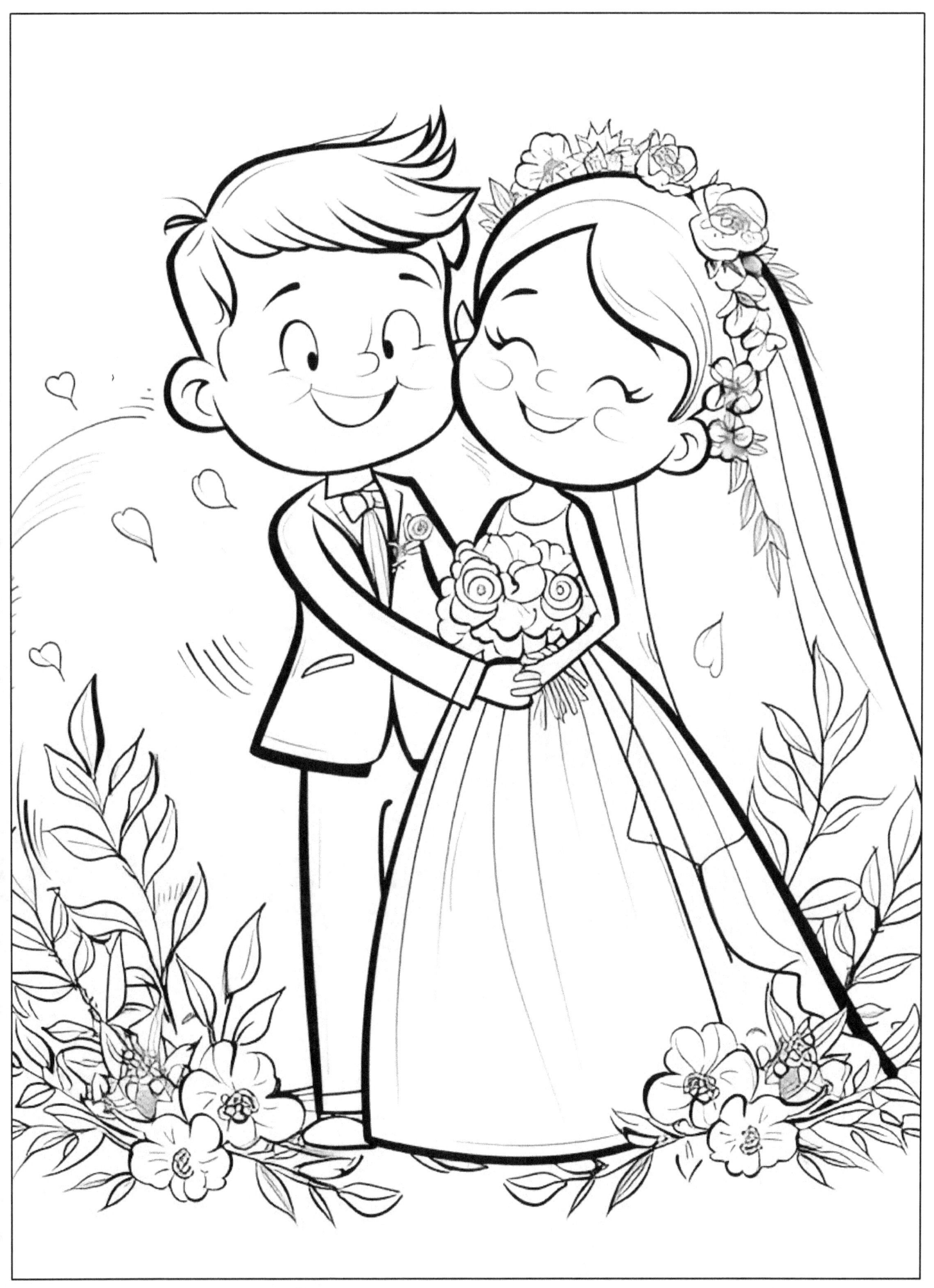

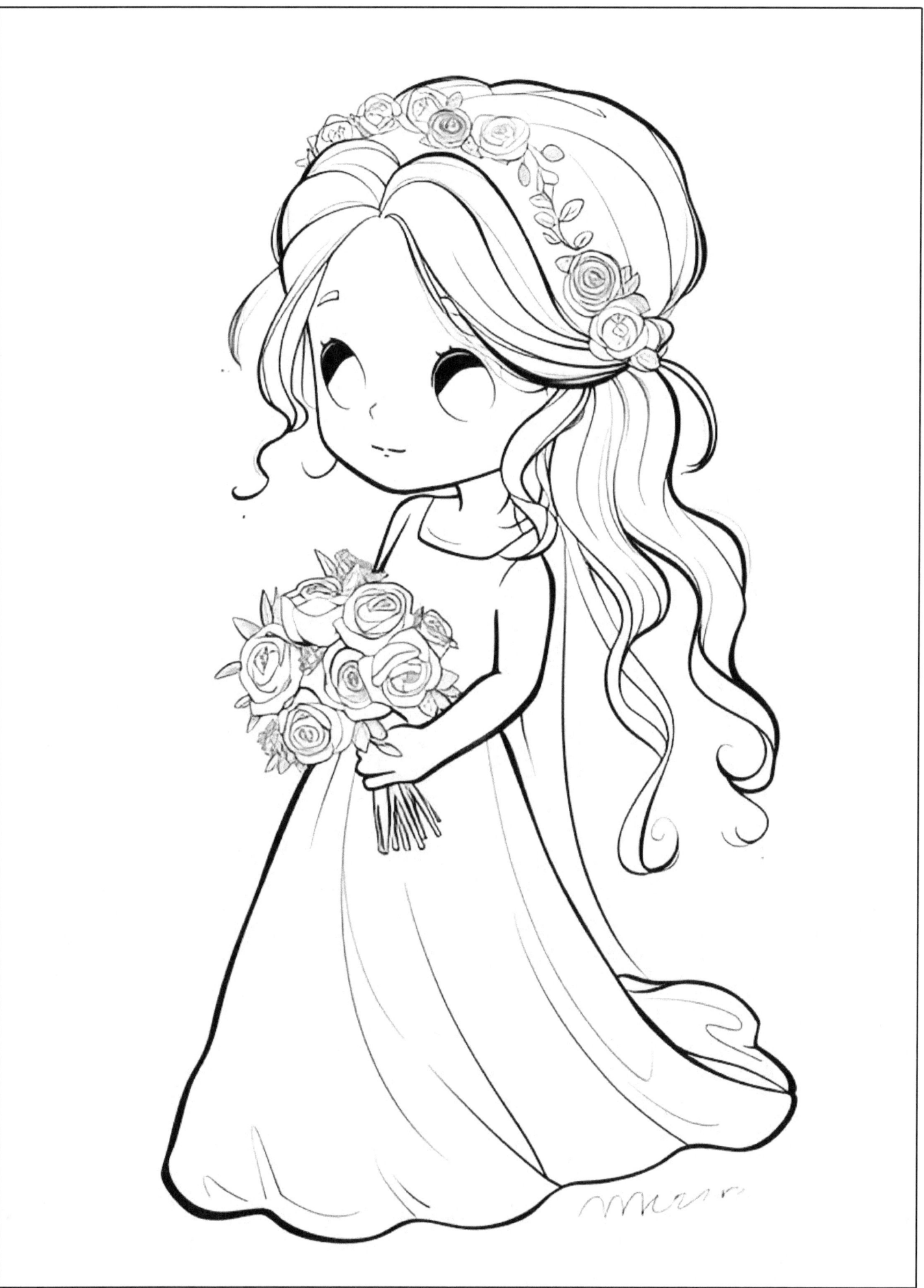

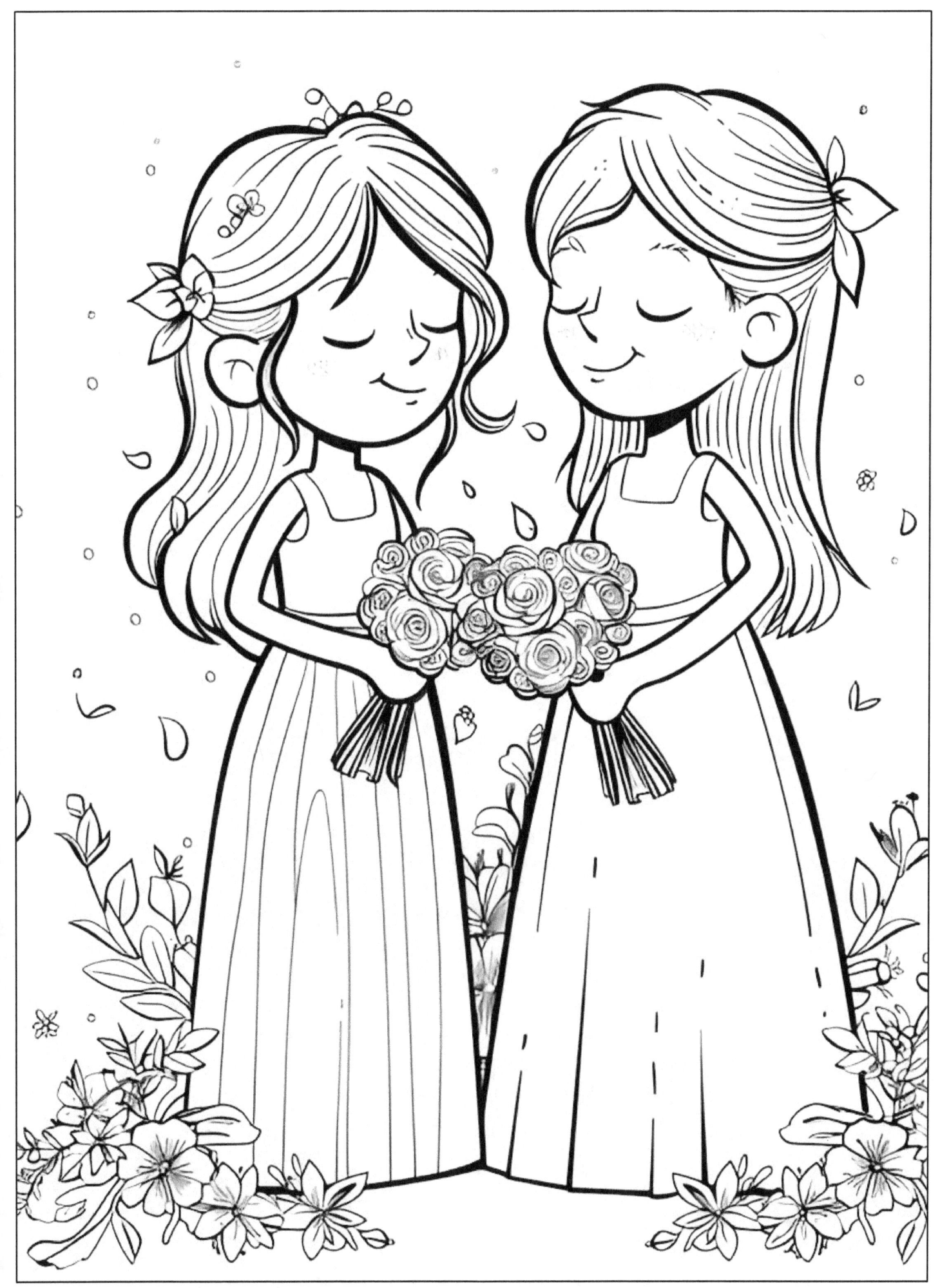

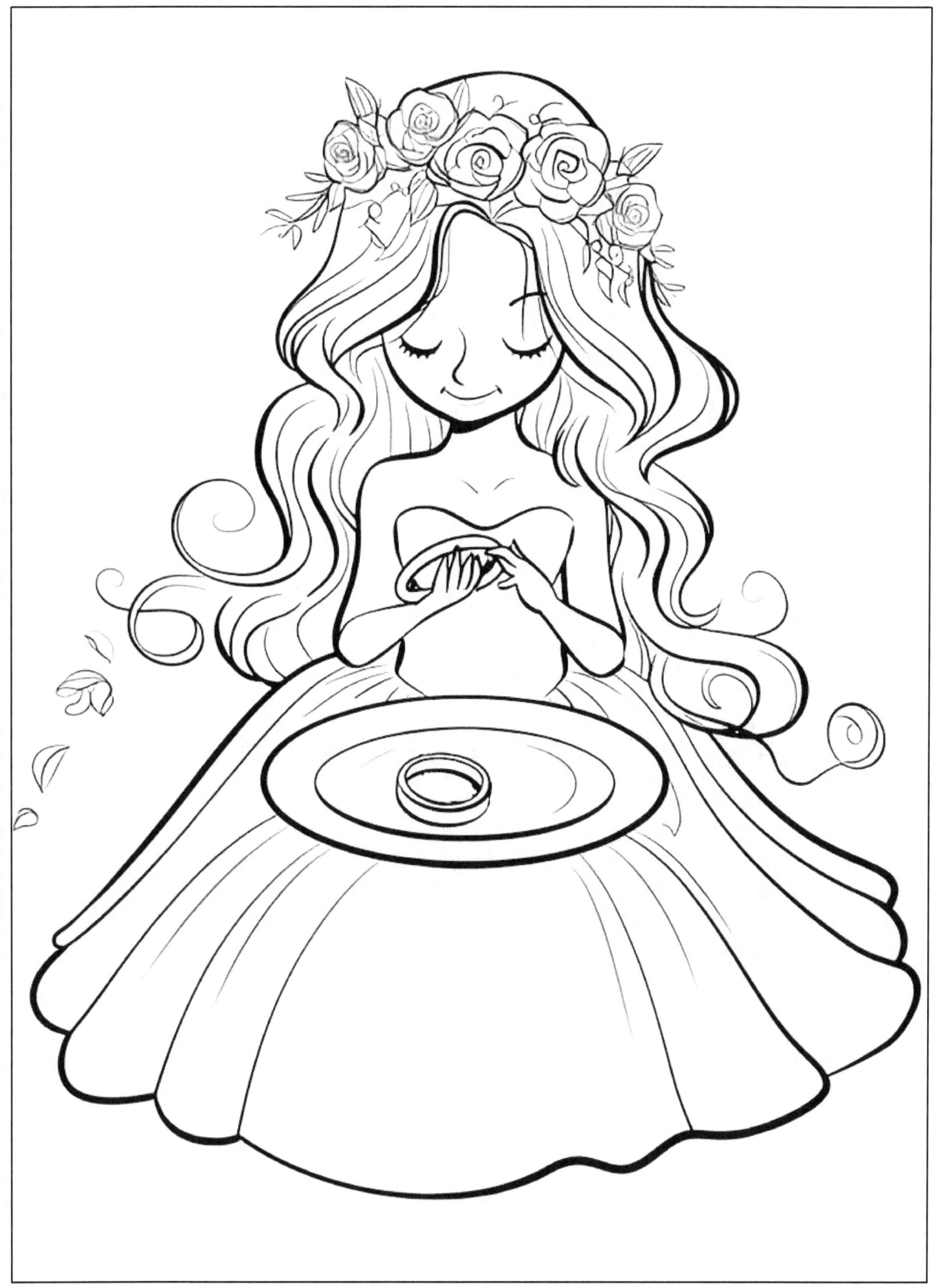

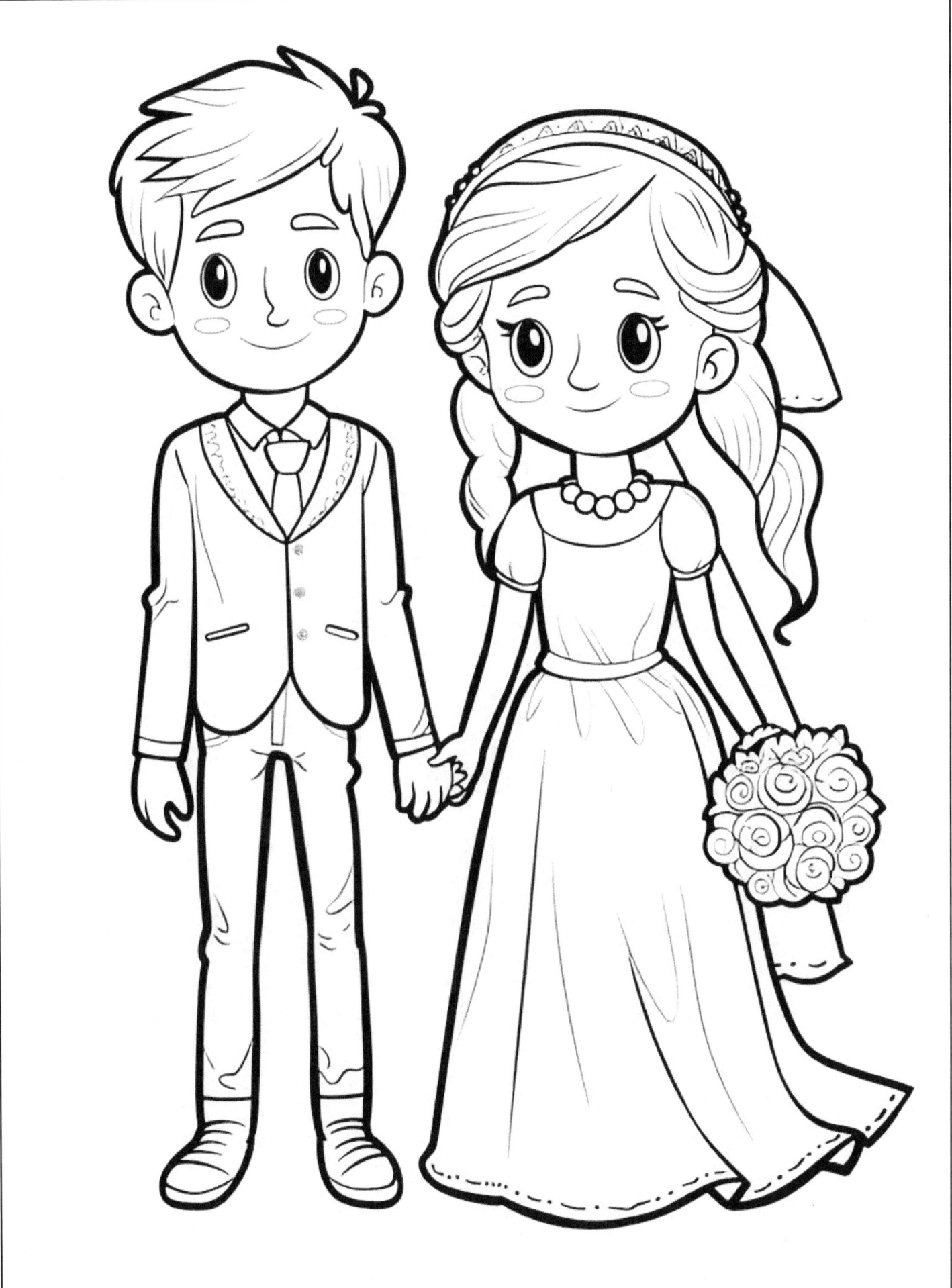

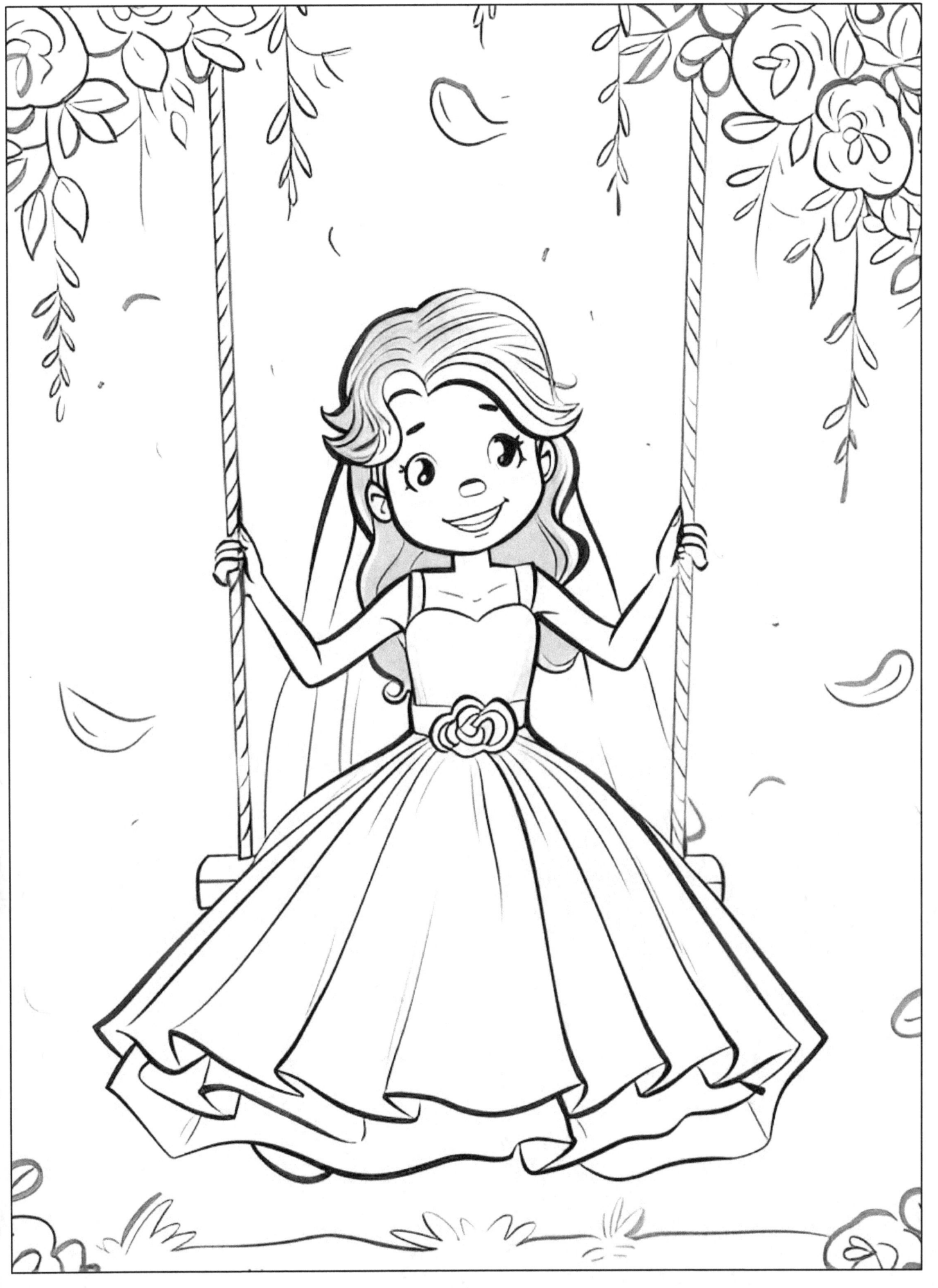

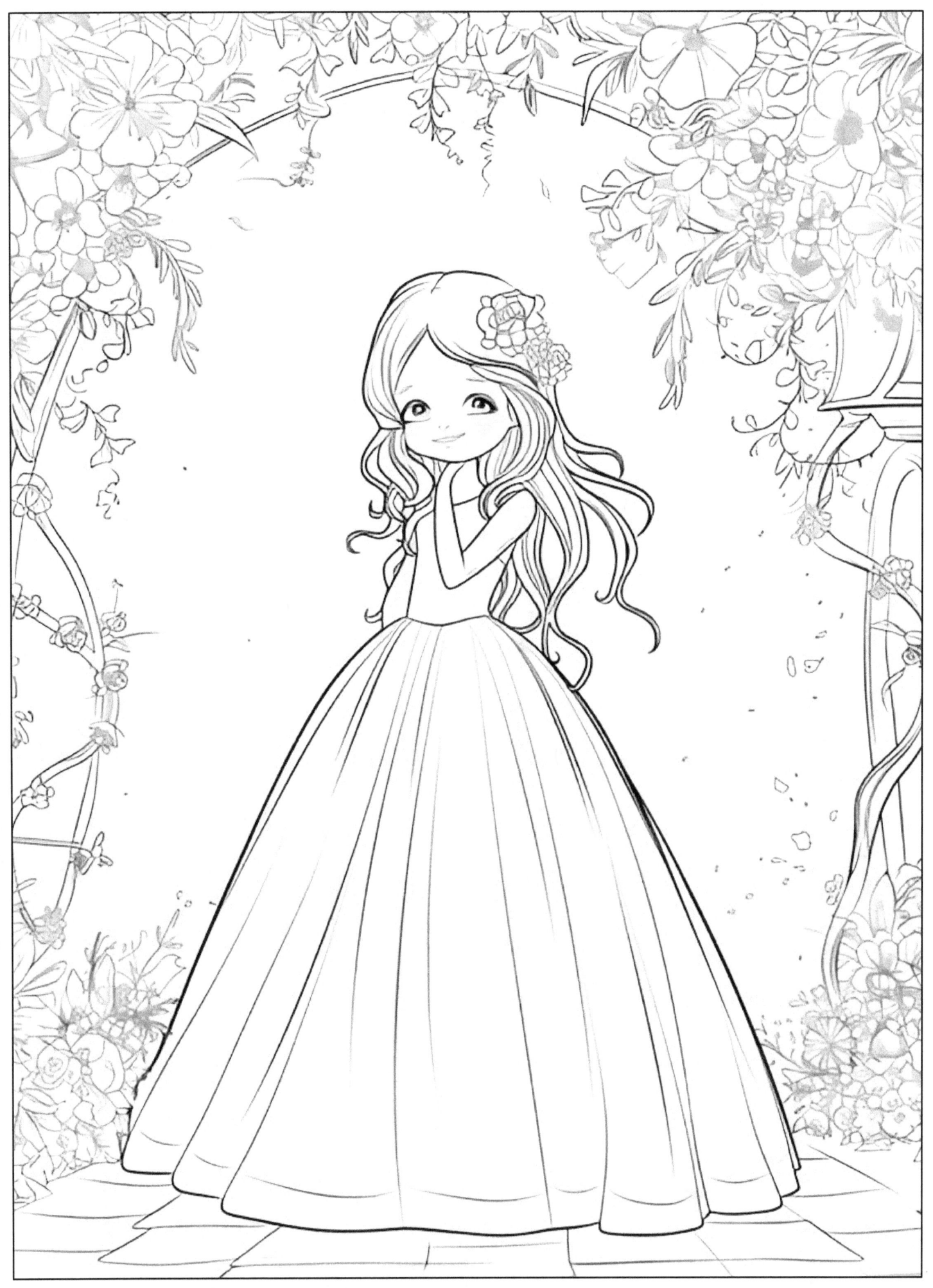

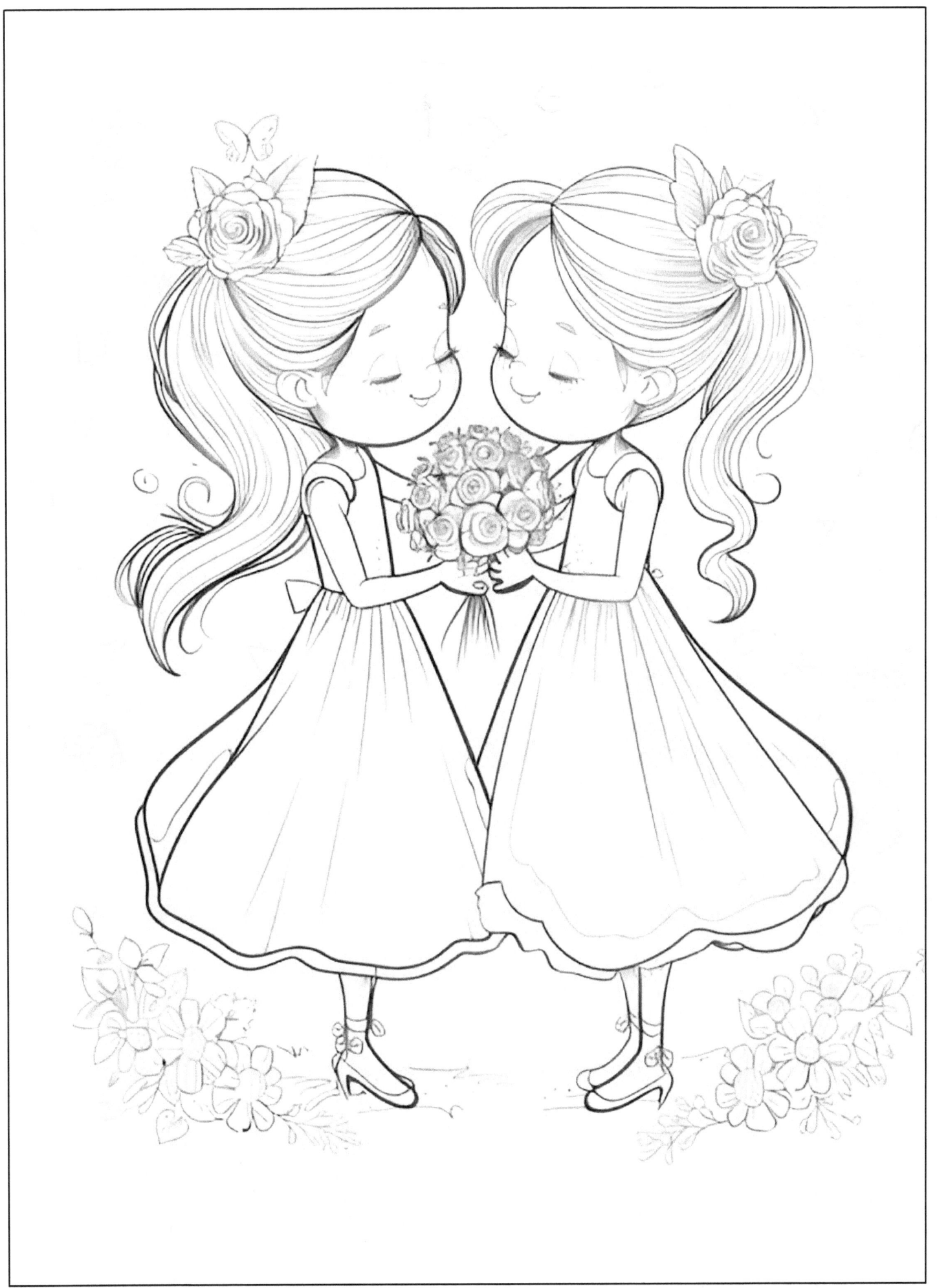

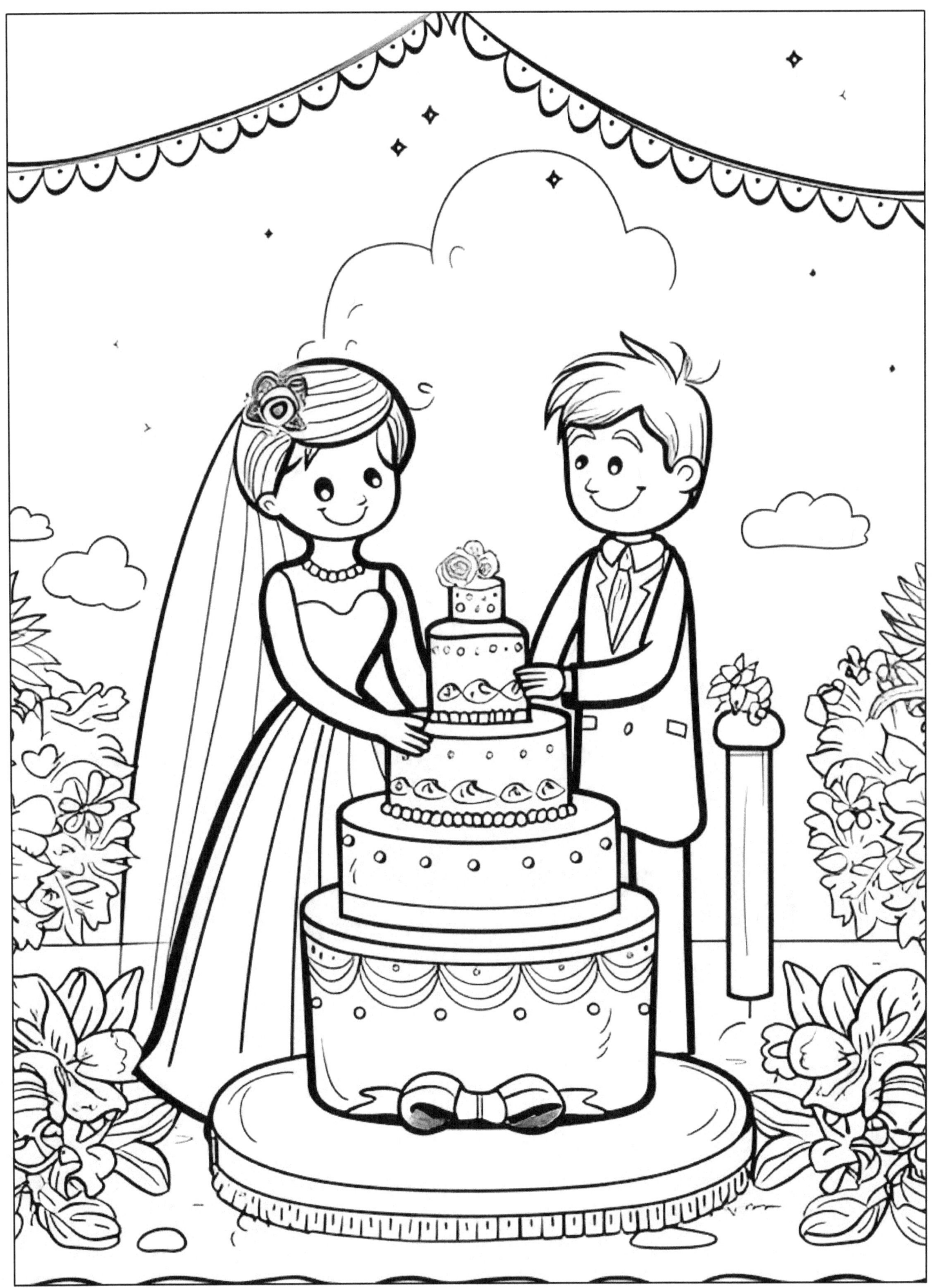

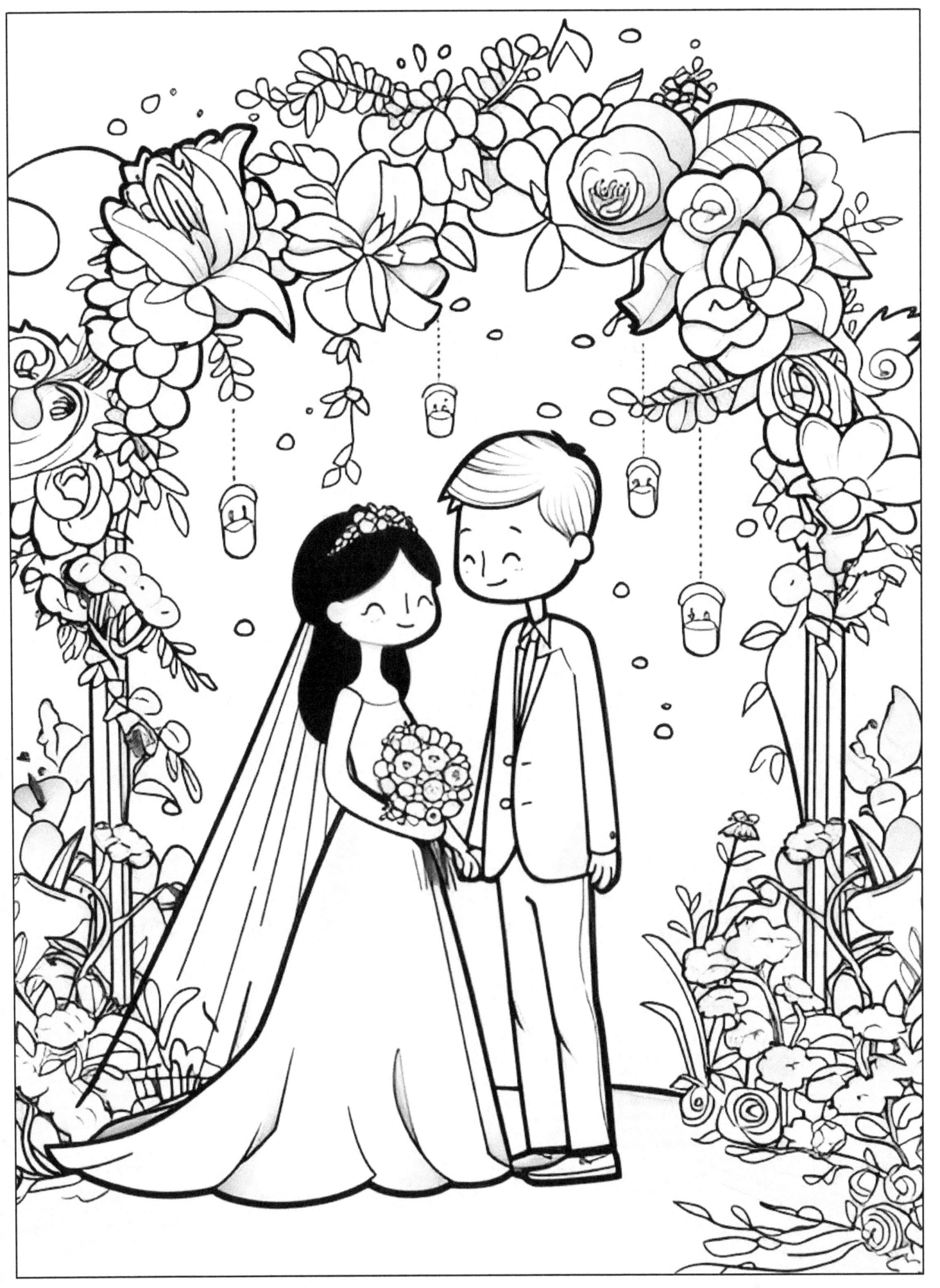

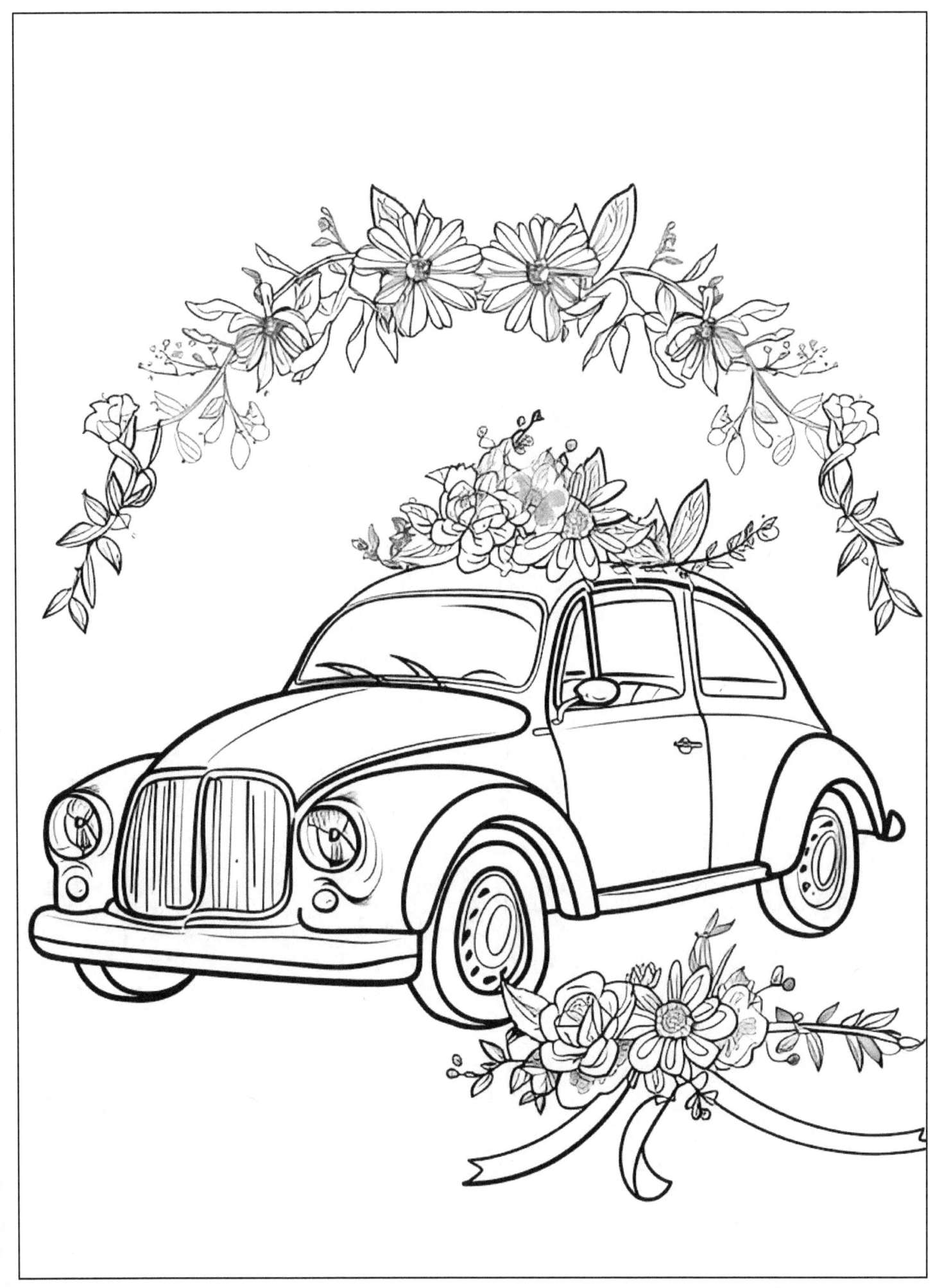

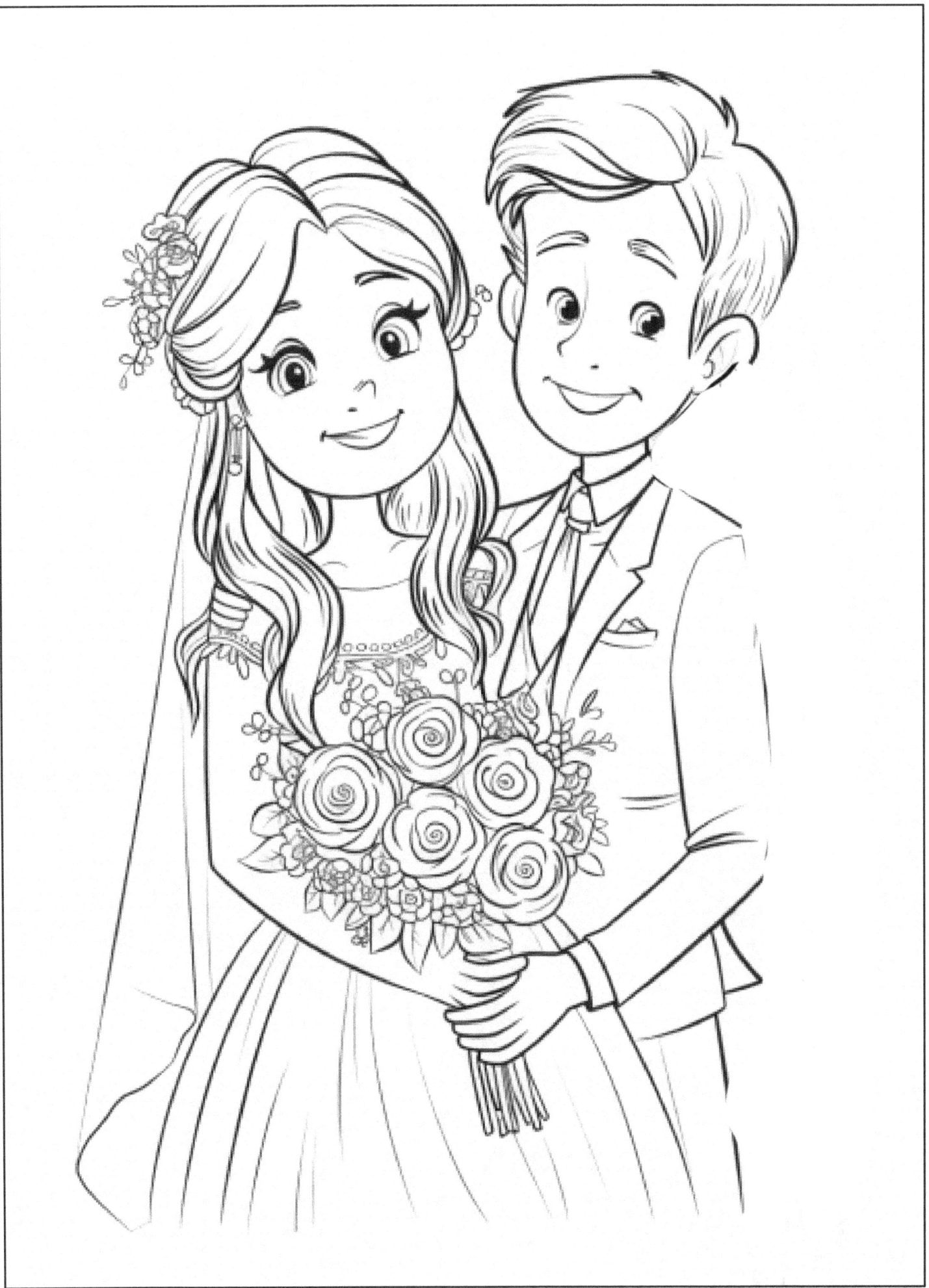